# THE JUGGLING BOOK

*For Val, John and Karen Hackett (PH)*
*For Joe Owen (PO)*

# THE
# JUGGLING
# BOOK

PHIL HACKETT • PETER OWEN

ILLUSTRATIONS BY STUART TROTTER

Lyons & Burford, Publishers

Printed in the United States of America

Design by Peter Owen
Illustrations by Stuart Trotter

10 9 8 7 6 5 4 3 2 1

Library of Congress Cataloging-in-Publication Data

Hackett, Phil.
    The juggling book / Phil Hackett, Peter Owen; illustrations by Stuart Trotter.
        p.    cm.
    Includes index.
    ISBN 1-55821-326-0
    1. Juggling.   I. Owen, Peter, 1950–   .   II. Trotter, Stuart.   III. Title.
GV1588.H33    1997
793.8'7—dc21                                                          97-130
                                                                      CIP

# CONTENTS

# INTRODUCTION

Although juggling has experienced a huge increase in popularity over the last few years, it is far from a modern phenomenon. Historians inform us that there is evidence to suggest that the Romans, American Indians and the Ancient Egyptians all had jugglers among their number. Pictures depicting jugglers exist that are almost four thousand years old!

What is juggling? The dictionary definition states that to juggle is to "perform feats of dexterity especially by tossing objects in the air and catching them, keeping several objects in the air at the same time." In addition to the traditional balls, clubs and rings, it is now generally accepted that the manipulation of the diabolo (a plastic, rubber, or wooden spool that is spun on a string tied between two hand sticks then flicked into the air and caught back on the string) and devil stick (a stick that is manipulated by tapping back and forth with two hand sticks giving the impression of the devil stick defying the laws of gravity) come within this definition. This book, however, will focus on the manipulation of balls and clubs. Once the basic patterns have been mastered they can easily be applied to rings or any other objects you wish to juggle. The best jugglers can juggle up to twelve objects at any one time. Combine the information in this book with positive thinking and practice and you too can gain incredible skills that will delight and amaze.

You may well be asking yourself a number of questions. Will I be able to juggle? Why would I want to juggle? If you can throw and catch one ball, then you can juggle. Don't believe people who claim they are "too uncoordinated" to learn to juggle. Success comes from positive thinking and practice; it is not some inherited gift. If you can't throw and catch one ball then keep on practicing — you **WILL** be able to juggle.

Why juggle? Well, first and most importantly it is tremendous fun! The satisfaction that is gained from conquering a new trick is motivation enough for most people. However, the benefits of juggling are numerous.

When you have learned the basics, juggling is very relaxing — just switch off and get lost in the patterns. Juggling provides exercise, improves motor skills and enhances the mind. Juggling teaches you to solve problems by breaking down insurmountable tasks into manageable portions. It is addictive and can be done all day or in a five-minute break from work — just slip three juggling balls into a bag or your pockets and juggle everywhere! Like learning to swim or riding a bicycle, it is impossible to forget! Juggling can and will improve the quality of your life.

## ———— How to Use This Book ————

This book is designed to teach you the basics of juggling, and then build upon your skills by introducing a whole repertoire of tricks. Within each section, the tricks have been rated on a five-star scale, tricks with five stars representing a particularly tough move. Bear in mind with all juggling moves that not everyone will progress at the same rate: Some people conquer moves quickly and with ease, others may take a little longer. Move at your own pace, and if you really want to juggle, it will happen! Five-star moves are difficult, and don't be surprised if they take a long time to master. Sometimes intermittent efforts over a year or more are required to achieve these particular tricks.

Three balls, two stars          Three clubs, two stars

Once you have mastered the basic patterns, in general it is best to work on a number of tricks during your practice time rather than decide that you want to master one trick before moving on. Why not work on five balls while practicing three clubs and the three ball Mills' Mess? You will be surprised how you suddenly start achieving goals that seemed far out of reach. When practicing tricks, don't just try them at the recommended heights. Vary the strength of your throws. This will improve your technique and make your patterns more "solid."

## Guide to Learning a New Trick

Information on the juggling equipment you will require is given at the start of each section.

First read all the pages relevant to the trick you are attempting, don't be over ambitious, learn the basic patterns. Pay particular attention to the tips and hints section, as it may well detail a practice move for you to try before you start work on the main trick.

One of your first questions might be: "Which hand do you throw the first ball or club with?" The answer is the one you find most comfortable, which is usually your dominant hand. With most people this will bring to light how uncoordinated your subordinate hand is, and initially throwing and catching will prove difficult. This will noticeably improve the more you juggle. Some juggling tricks are not balanced: For example, in the three-ball half shower every ball from the right is shown being thrown over the top of the pattern. With this type of trick you may prefer to swap right for left, particularly if your dominant hand is your left hand. Whichever way you learn these unbalanced tricks, you should go on to master them both ways as this will open up a whole range of possible variations.

The balls or clubs are numbered in the step-by-step diagrams, partly to help you trace their patterns, but in many tricks the numbers also demonstrate the order of release. The direction, path and recommended height of a throw is clearly indicated with arrows and guide lines. Rarely are new tricks achieved without problems, so a troubleshooting section highlights the most common problems and faults. If a problem persists, stop, breakdown the move into sections and analyze each section.

# 1

# BALL JUGGLING

## —————— Three-Ball Juggling ——————

To get started and make your first moves, you will need three balls, but please don't assume that any three balls will be suitable. The ideal ball for juggling is actually called a *beanbag*. You may well have a local store that stocks juggling equipment, but in addition to juggling specialists, toy stores, sports stores and gift stores may also sell a range of equipment.

Buy a set of three round beanbags that are about the size of a tennis ball and weigh approximately seven ounces (180 grams), heavy enough for your hand to close around them naturally when they drop into it. A beanbag has the advantage of being easy to catch and not rolling away when dropped. There is also another great advantage to beanbags in that they are manufactured in a wide range of colors. Buy three different colors and this will make it easier to trace the path of each individual ball.

If you are not able to buy juggling balls then do not despair! Any hard ball such as a baseball will be about the right weight (but you will have to chase it when it hits the ground). Please don't try using tennis balls, as they are so light that they make juggling very difficult.

Now that you have the right equipment you are ready to take your first steps toward juggling success ...

# THREE-BALL CASCADE

*Skill Rating*

The three-ball cascade is one of the most basic and rhythmic of juggling patterns. It is easy to learn, has many variations and is the pattern that jugglers often return to in between tricks. It is the ideal pattern to start you juggling.

Shown over the next few pages are the seven main steps to learn the cascade. You will start gently with only one ball and steadily work up to three. Don't forget: move at your own pace, be confident with each step before moving onto the next step, and you will juggle!

Here are two important tips to successful juggling:

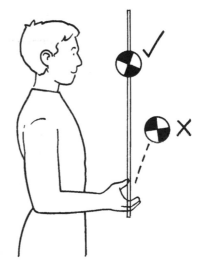

● Juggling within an imaginary box, with a midline, helps to ensure your throws go to a consistent height and do not go out too wide.

● Make sure balls are kept within an imaginary flat plane in front of you. Adjust errant throws by altering the angle of your wrists.

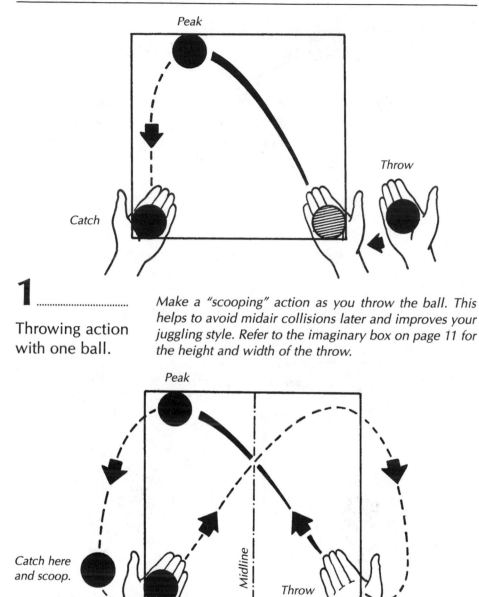

# 1

## Throwing action with one ball.

*Make a "scooping" action as you throw the ball. This helps to avoid midair collisions later and improves your juggling style. Refer to the imaginary box on page 11 for the height and width of the throw.*

# 2

## Figure-of-eight with one ball.

*This shows the path that all the balls follow in the cascade. Concentrate on smooth scoops, consistent height and width, and rhythm. Master this figure-of-eight throw before attempting two balls.*

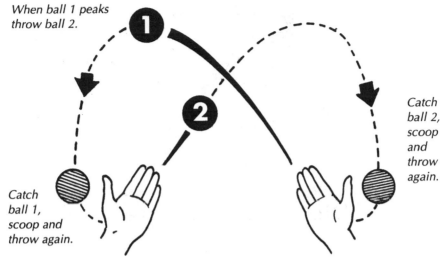

When ball 1 peaks throw ball 2.

Catch ball 2, scoop and throw again.

Catch ball 1, scoop and throw again.

# 3 ..............................

## Throwing action with two balls.

*This is the key to three-ball juggling — being accurate with two balls. Throw ball 1 and when it peaks throw ball 2 to the same height. If the two balls land in your hands almost simultaneously then you are not throwing to the same height. Try to keep the balls going around in the figure-of-eight pattern but remember at this stage it won't be a continuous flow, it will be throw-throw, catch-catch, stop, throw-throw etc.*

Subordinate hand

Dominant hand

# 4 ..............................

## Start position for three balls.

*Before moving onto juggling three balls, you will need to be able to adopt the start position. Practice holding the balls as shown above, and in particular note how the dominant hand holds two balls.*

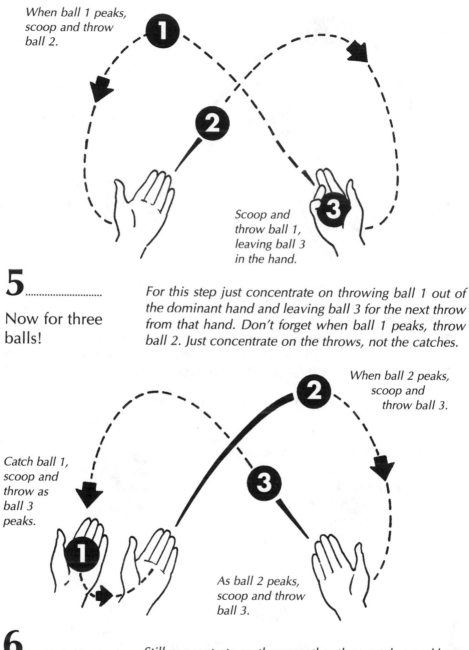

When ball 1 peaks, scoop and throw ball 2.

Scoop and throw ball 1, leaving ball 3 in the hand.

When ball 2 peaks, scoop and throw ball 3.

Catch ball 1, scoop and throw as ball 3 peaks.

As ball 2 peaks, scoop and throw ball 3.

# 5............................

## Now for three balls!

*For this step just concentrate on throwing ball 1 out of the dominant hand and leaving ball 3 for the next throw from that hand. Don't forget when ball 1 peaks, throw ball 2. Just concentrate on the throws, not the catches.*

# 6............................

## Throwing action with three balls.

*Still concentrate on throws rather than catches and keep your eyes fixed on top of the pattern. When ball 2 peaks, throw ball 3 and catch ball 1 with your subordinate hand. Don't forget to "scoop and throw."*

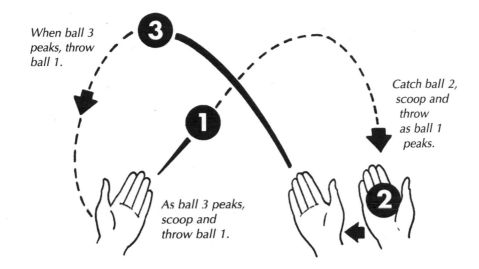

When ball 3 peaks, throw ball 1.

Catch ball 2, scoop and throw as ball 1 peaks.

As ball 3 peaks, scoop and throw ball 1.

# 7
.........................

## Juggling with three balls.

*It is unlikely to work immediately so just keep trying! Don't think of each ball as different or as a numbered ball, just throw a ball whenever the previous one peaks. Get the throws right and the catches will take care of themselves; your brain will learn to adjust your hands according to the trajectory of the balls.*

NOW JUST KEEP THROWING!
Remember: every time one ball peaks, throw another. Rhythm is an important part of juggling, so as your action starts to smooth out and improve, concentrate on keeping a steady rhythm.

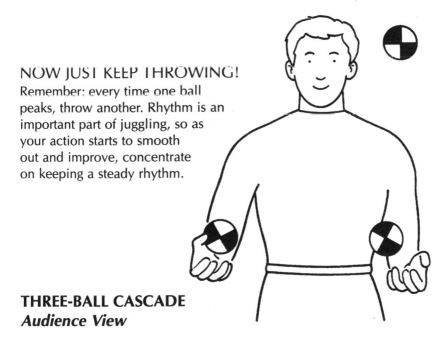

## THREE-BALL CASCADE
### *Audience View*

# OVER THE TOP

**Basic Move**

*Skill Rating*

**1** *While cascading ...*
Move your right hand
(complete with ball)
farther out to the
right than usual
for cascading.

**2** Launch ball 1 clearly
over the top of the
other balls.

**3** Bring hand back for
incoming ball.

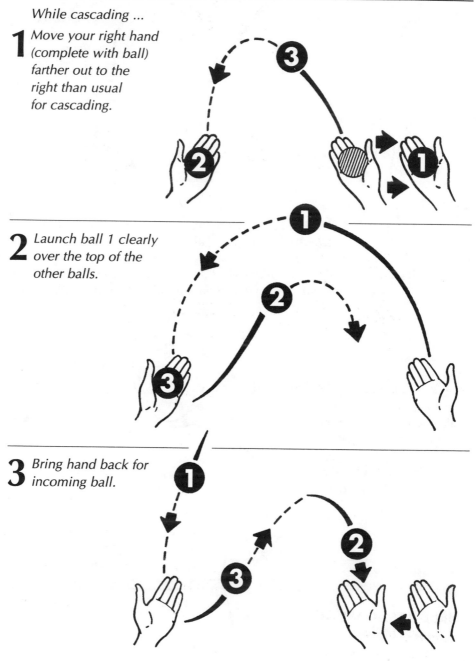

## OVER THE TOP *Audience View*

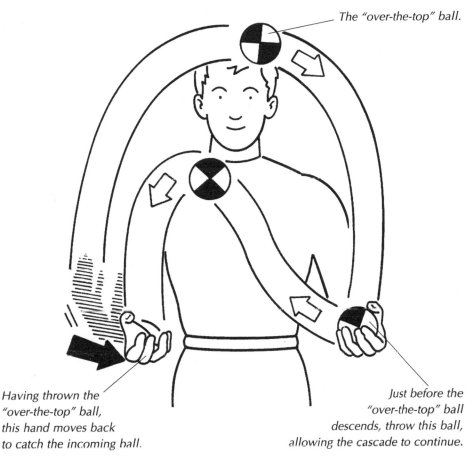

*The "over-the-top" ball.*

*Having thrown the "over-the-top" ball, this hand moves back to catch the incoming ball.*

*Just before the "over-the-top" ball descends, throw this ball, allowing the cascade to continue.*

| TROUBLESHOOTING |
| --- |

● If the ball destined to go over the top collides with another ball, you haven't moved your hand far enough out to the side.

| TIPS AND HINTS |
| --- |

● Try throwing the "over-the-top" ball to different heights. If you throw this ball high, then wait for a moment with one ball in each hand. Just before the high ball descends (to be caught by the left hand), throw the ball in the left hand, allowing the cascade to continue.

### The next challenge:
Work on an over-the-top throw from the left hand.

## OVER THE TOP *Tricks*

### The Half Shower

*Every throw from one hand goes over the top. Balls follow this pattern instead of a figure-of-eight pattern. Once you have mastered one way, reverse it, and try it the other way.*

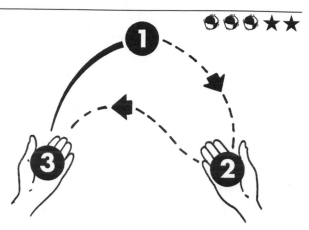

### Tennis

*Throw ball 1 over the top from the right, and then when it lands throw it back over the top while doing normal (cascade) throws with balls 2 and 3. It helps (and looks better) for the "tennis" ball (ball 1) to be a different color from the other two.*

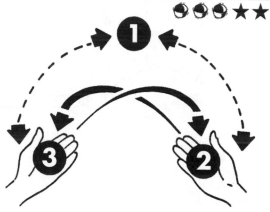

### The Reverse Cascade

*Every ball is thrown from the outside of the pattern over the top into the **center** of the pattern and not to the other side of the pattern as with the above tricks. Your hands collect the incoming balls from the center and move outward to throw.*

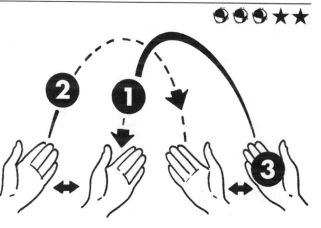

# COLUMNS

**Basic Move**

*Skill Rating*

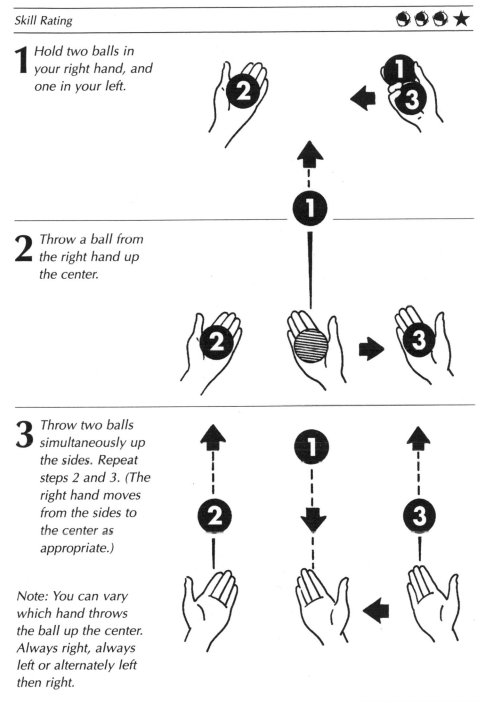

**1** Hold two balls in
your right hand, and
one in your left.

**2** Throw a ball from
the right hand up
the center.

**3** Throw two balls
simultaneously up
the sides. Repeat
steps 2 and 3. (The
right hand moves
from the sides to
the center as
appropriate.)

Note: You can vary
which hand throws
the ball up the center.
Always right, always
left or alternately left
then right.

## COLUMNS *Audience View*

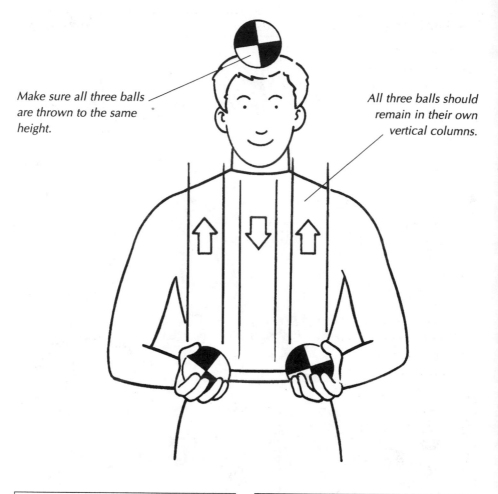

*Make sure all three balls are thrown to the same height.*

*All three balls should remain in their own vertical columns.*

---

### TROUBLESHOOTING

● As long as you have first practiced throwing two balls to the same height, you shouldn't have any difficulties with this trick.

● Concentrate on a steady tick-tock rhythm.

### *The next challenge:*

### TIPS AND HINTS

● Practice simultaneously throwing two balls to the same height and catching them before working on the trick. When introducing the third ball, concentrate on keeping the balls in their own vertical columns, at the same height.

Instead of throwing the "lone" ball up the inside, try throwing it up the right-hand side. Done that? How about the left-hand side?

## COLUMNS *Tricks*

### The Umbrella (or Rainbow Cross)

*First practice throwing two balls simultaneously, but so they cross in the center. Now try the columns rhythm with three balls but the two outside balls crossing. Throw ball 3 slightly higher than ball 2 to avoid collisions.*

### Figure-of-Eight

*The center ball, ball 1, weaves a figure-of-eight pattern around the other two balls.*

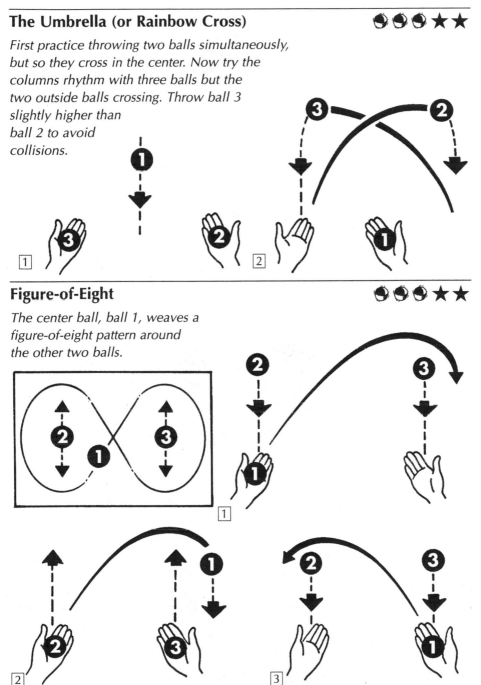

# UNDER-THE-ARM THROW

*Basic Move*

*Skill Rating*

1. *While cascading at about head height, release a ball from your left hand.*

2. *Immediately move your right arm to the left so that the wrist of your right hand is directly below the left wrist.*

3. *Launch the ball upward in a straight line.*

**4** *Your right hand returns rapidly to its normal position, and your left hand throws and then moves to the left slightly to collect the ball thrown under the arm.*

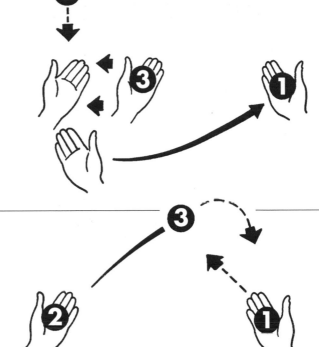

**5** *Your left hand returns to its usual position, and the cascade resumes.*

## UNDER-THE-ARM THROW *Audience View*

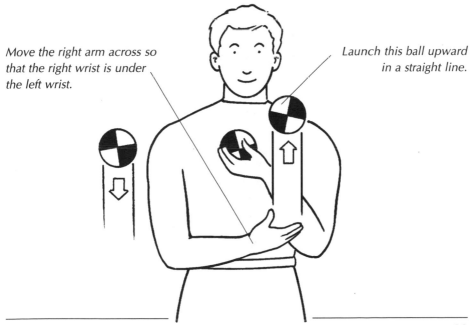

*Move the right arm across so that the right wrist is under the left wrist.*

*Launch this ball upward in a straight line.*

## TROUBLESHOOTING

● If you are dropping the ball that is marked *1* on the diagram, then you are probably not moving your right arm across (step 2) early enough.

### *The next challenge:*
Try throwing under the other arm.

## TIPS AND HINTS

● To ensure the throw always goes under the arm, do not move your left arm toward your chest. Hold the left hand clearly out in front of you and move the right arm under the left wrist.

## UNDER-THE-ARM THROW *Tricks*

### Continuous Under-the-Arm

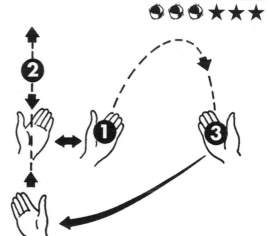

*Try throwing every single ball from one hand under the opposite arm, in this case the throw with the right under the left. Focus on keeping the throws from the right hand vertical and small movements of the left hand backward and forward.*

### Upside-Down Tennis

*Throw a ball under one arm, then the same ball under the other. This ball always get thrown under alternate arms while the others are cascaded as normal.*

### Under-the-Leg

*Follow the steps outlined for Under-the-Arm: instead of throwing under your left wrist, lift your left leg high and throw the ball in the right hand deep under your leg. It helps to throw the ball before (the one from the left hand) higher than normal to give you more time, and also to move your left leg to the right slightly while throwing the ball.*

# THREE-BALL SHOWER

**Basic Move**

*Skill Rating*

*Steps: First learn the preliminary move described in Tips and Hints (page 26).*

**1** Hold two balls in your right hand, and one in your left hand.

**2** Throw ball 1 from the right hand to about head height to the left.

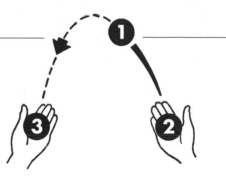

**3** Simultaneously throw ball 2 from your right hand toward the left and "spring" ball 3 from your left hand horizontally across to your right hand.

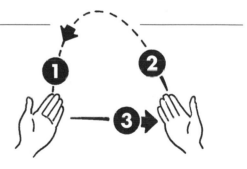

**4** Catch ball 1 in your left hand.

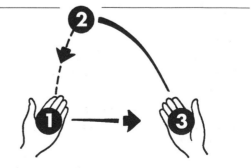

*Repeat steps 3 and 4 to keep the shower going.*

## THREE-BALL SHOWER *Audience View*

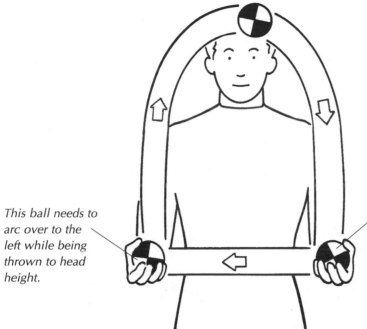

This ball needs to arc over to the left while being thrown to head height.

At exactly the same time as the ball from the right hand is being thrown, "spring" this ball from the left hand to the right hand.

| TROUBLESHOOTING |
| :---: |

● If you are having problems, practice the move described in Tips and Hints some more. Don't try to do this move continuously : do it once; stop; do it again.

● Concentrate on making sure your throws from your right hand aren't going up straight, but are arcing to the left.

| TIPS AND HINTS |
| :---: |

● Practice this as a two-ball move before trying the three-ball trick.

● Hold a ball in your right hand and a ball in your left. **Simultaneously**, throw the right-hand ball to the left at head height and "spring" the ball in your left hand horizontally to your right hand.

● These things **must** happen at the same time as one move.

### The next challenge:

Try and go into the shower from a cascade, then go back to the cascade.
To go from the cascade to the shower, throw a high ball from the right and go straight in.

## THREE-BALL SHOWER *Tricks*

### The Reverse Shower ★★★★

*The shower in the opposite direction can be very difficult. Just spend a lot of time practicing the preliminary move, as described in Tips and Hints, then go for it! The effort will be worthwhile, as it allows you access to the two super tricks below.*

### The Box / The Seesaw ★★★★★

*This is a challenging trick that is essentially alternate showers. The only difference is the balls at the side — ball 1 and ball 3 — must not arc, but go straight up and down as if outlining the sides of a box.*

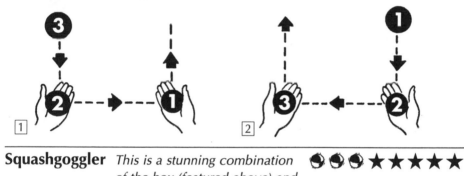

**Squashgoggler** *This is a stunning combination of the box (featured above) and juggling two balls in one hand (see fig.1,left hand). Once mastered it looks best low and fast.* ★★★★★

# DUMMY ELEVATOR

*Basic Move*

*Skill Rating*

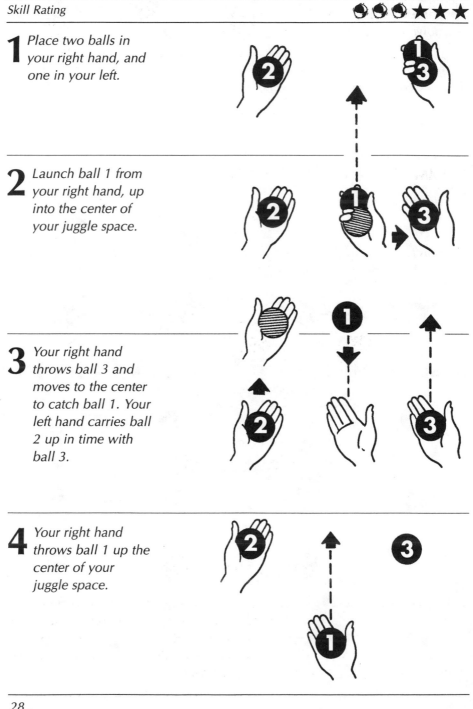

**1** Place two balls in your right hand, and one in your left.

**2** Launch ball 1 from your right hand, up into the center of your juggle space.

**3** Your right hand throws ball 3 and moves to the center to catch ball 1. Your left hand carries ball 2 up in time with ball 3.

**4** Your right hand throws ball 1 up the center of your juggle space.

**5** *Your left hand carries ball 2 back down as ball 3 falls.*

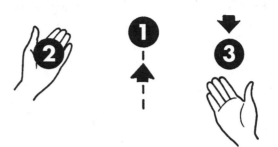

## DUMMY ELEVATOR  *Audience View*

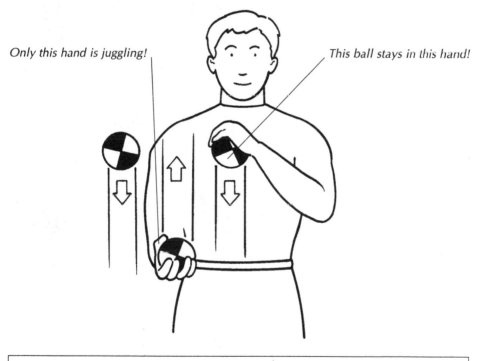

*Only this hand is juggling!*

*This ball stays in this hand!*

---

### *TROUBLESHOOTING*

● The most common error is to drop the balls in your right hand as you raise your left. Practice holding the left ball at head height while keeping two balls going in your right hand. Then try moving the left hand randomly as you juggle two in your right. Eventually you will have no problem co-ordinating the rising of ball 3 and your left hand.

## TIPS AND HINTS

● Practice juggling two balls in your right hand before introducing the third ball. Concentrate on keeping the balls (ball 1 and ball 3) in their own vertical columns, and throwing them both to the same height.

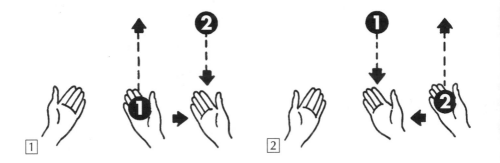

### *The next challenge:*
Try moving your left hand, and of course ball 2, in time with ball 1 (the center ball).

## DUMMY ELEVATOR *Tricks*

### Alternate Dummies

*Relearn the dummy elevator with your right hand carrying the ball, then alternate the hand that carries, first left then right.*

# BACK CROSSES

*Basic Move*

*Skill Rating*

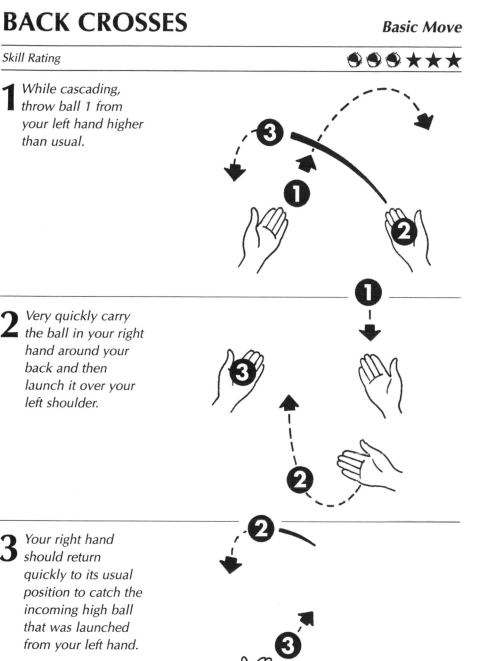

**1** While cascading, throw ball 1 from your left hand higher than usual.

**2** Very quickly carry the ball in your right hand around your back and then launch it over your left shoulder.

**3** Your right hand should return quickly to its usual position to catch the incoming high ball that was launched from your left hand.

# BACK CROSSES *Audience View*

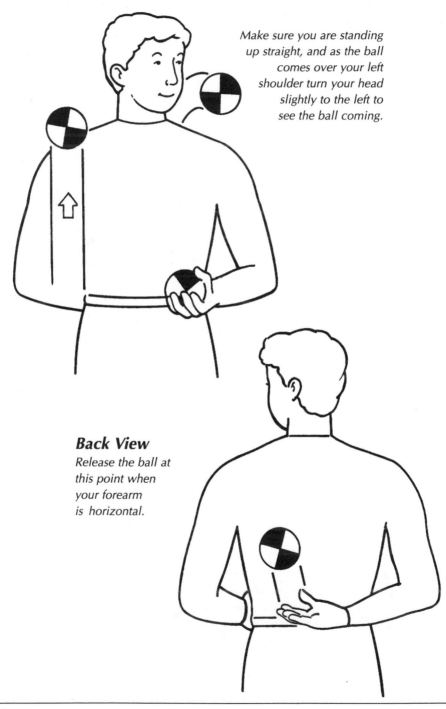

*Make sure you are standing up straight, and as the ball comes over your left shoulder turn your head slightly to the left to see the ball coming.*

## Back View
*Release the ball at this point when your forearm is horizontal.*

## TROUBLESHOOTING

● The most common problem is that the ball doesn't go over your shoulder correctly. It either flies too far forward or goes to the left or to the right after going over your shoulder. To ensure that you have the correct positioning for the ball, stand up straight and practice throwing a ball from your right hand over your left shoulder. Concentrate on releasing the ball when your forearm is horizontal. Do not consciously throw forward.

### The next challenge:
Try throwing every ball from your right hand over your left shoulder. Keep the throws from your left hand higher than usual.

## TIPS AND HINTS

● The ball should **feel** like it is being thrown straight up. If you do this, it will actually go forward and over your left shoulder the correct distance. As the ball comes over your left shoulder, turn your head left so that you can see the ball coming. If you don't do this it is almost impossible to catch the ball.

**Side View**

## BACK CROSSES *Tricks*

### Offside Back Cross                    ●●●★★★

*This trick is slightly more difficult than using the preferred hand. Simply swap left for right in the above instructions.*

### Solid Back Crosses                    ●●●★★★★★

*Not an easy trick! Every ball thrown goes over the opposite shoulder to the hand that threw it. Keep your throws fairly high above your head to make the trick slow, and be sure not to rush the throws too much, otherwise the balls will be released at the wrong moment and fly everywhere. Tilt your head backward and look straight up, only moving your eyes left and right as the balls come over your shoulders.*

# THE MACHINE

*Basic Move*

*Skill Rating*

1 *Launch ball 1 from your right hand, up the center of your juggle space.*

2 *Launch ball 3 vertically from your right hand, and carry ball 2 in your left hand in time with ball 3.*

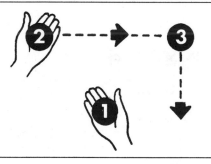

3 *Move your right hand to the center of your juggle space to catch ball 1.*

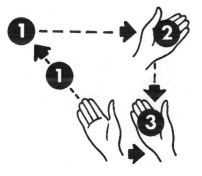

4 *Launch ball 1 slightly to the left from your right hand. Move your right hand to the right to catch ball 3. Your left hand carries ball 2 in a straight line across the top of the pattern.*

**5** *Ball 2 is dropped by your left hand on the far right of the pattern. Your left hand returns to the left swiftly and claws ball 1 from the air. Ball 3 is launched up the center of your juggle space from your right hand. Your left hand carries ball 1 down. Your right hand moves to the right to catch ball 2.*

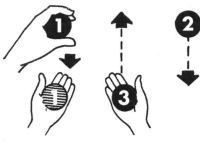

*Your position is now similar to that shown in step 2 (although the actual balls have changed places).*

*Repeat steps 2 to 5 to continue the pattern.*

## THE MACHINE  *Audience View*

*Drop this ball and quickly move your hand back to claw the next ball on the left-hand side.*

*This ball, from the right hand, must be thrown over to the left-hand side of the juggle space.*

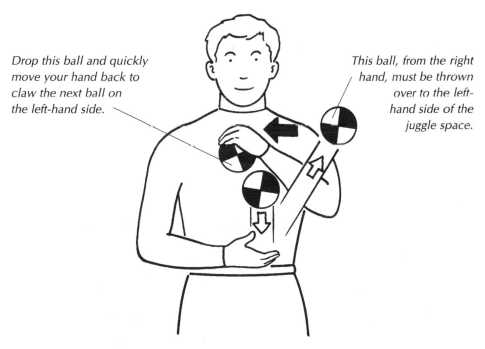

| TROUBLESHOOTING | TIPS AND HINTS |
|---|---|

● The most common error is to forget to throw the center ball slightly to the left as the left hand is moving over the top of the pattern. Concentrate on throwing ball 3 to the left from the right hand, and the quick return of the left hand after dropping the ball on the right-hand side.

● Practice moving your left hand above your juggle space while juggling the other two balls in your right hand. This trick looks fantastic if your left hand makes jerky movements, as if it were a robot arm. Very clearly go straight up and then straight across.

**The next challenge:**
For the brave, try reversing the whole trick by carrying with your right hand.

## THE MACHINE *Tricks*

### Continuous Machine

●●● ★ ★ ★ ★ ★ ★

*This trick looks great, but perseverance is required! Don't be surprised if you can only do this for a couple of throws even after months of practice. The balls travel in a right-angled triangular pattern. Your left hand plucks balls out of the pattern at head height and keeps pulling them across the top. Your left hand should stay at head height. The trick is actually a type of shower.*

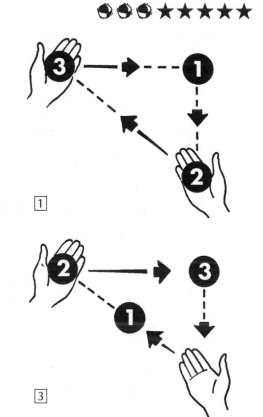

# MILLS' MESS

*Basic Move*

*Skill Rating*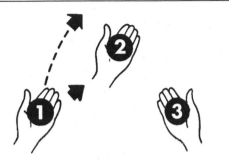

*From cascade:*

**1** *Your left hand throws ball 1 over the top of your juggle space.*

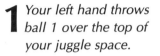

**2** *Your left hand carries ball 2 to the right of your juggle space, while your right hand moves under your left arm.*

**3** *Ball 1 falls **between** your crossed arms. Your right hand throws ball 3 almost vertically from under the left arm (your arms should be left over right).*

**4** *Your right hand moves a little to the right and catches ball 1.*

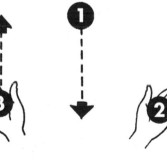

**5** *Your left hand tosses ball 2 toward the left, and quickly moves left itself to catch ball 3.*

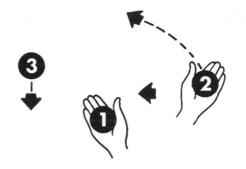

**6** *Your right hand throws ball 1 to the left, and carries ball 2 to the left of the juggle space; meanwhile your left arm moves right underneath your right arm.*

**7** *Ball 1 falls **between** your crossed arms. Your left hand throws ball 3 almost vertically from under your right arm (your arms should be right over left).*

**8** *Your left hand moves a little to the right and catches ball 1. Your right hand throws ball 2 to the right, and moves right to catch ball 3. Your left arm moves to the the left. Go back to step 1.*

## MILLS' MESS *Audience View*

*Three different-colored balls are a great advantage to learning this difficult pattern.*

*This ball should always fall between your crossed arms.*

---

### TROUBLESHOOTING

● Once you actually understand what's going on, the "Mess" isn't that difficult. However, throwing balls from the cross-arm position can feel odd, so why not practice cascading with your arms permanently crossed to get used to it?

● Also concentrate on making sure that ball 1 falls **between** your crossed arms.

### TIPS AND HINTS

● Notice that each ball has its own part to play. For example, ball 2 always gets carried through the center of the pattern. It's always ball 1 that is thrown over the top, and ball 3 always gets thrown under the arms. Use three different-colored balls—it will help you to sort out the pattern.

# THREE IN ONE HAND

**Basic Move**

*Skill Rating*

Hold balls in configuration as shown.

**1** Hold your hand slightly to the right of the center of your body. Launch ball 1 on a path **slightly** to the right.

**2** Launch ball 2 on a similar trajectory.

**3** Launch the last ball in your hand the same as ball 2. Move your hand to the right to catch the incoming ball.

**4** Move your hand to the left. Repeat steps 3 and 4 to keep the pattern going.

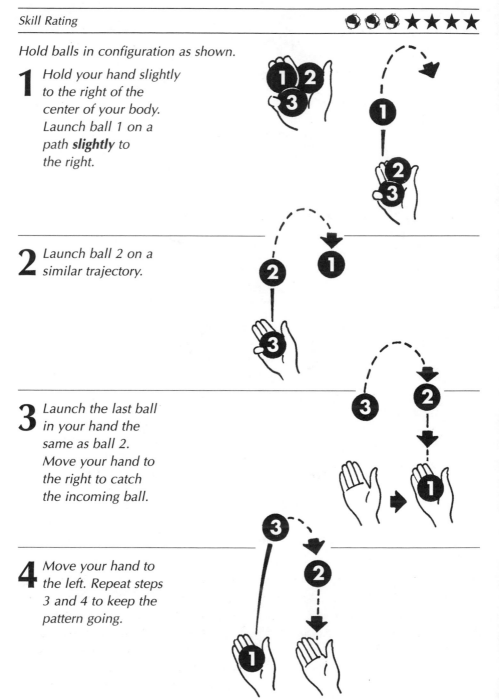

# THREE IN ONE HAND *Audience View*

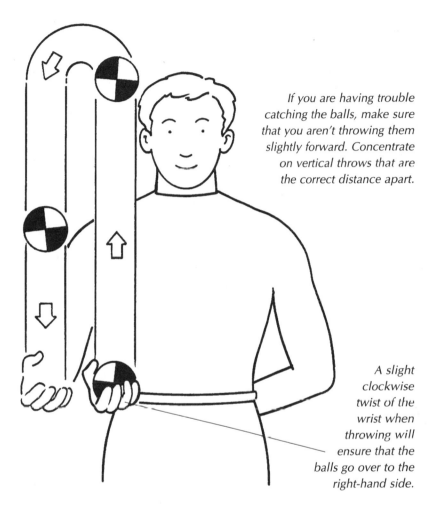

*If you are having trouble catching the balls, make sure that you aren't throwing them slightly forward. Concentrate on vertical throws that are the correct distance apart.*

*A slight clockwise twist of the wrist when throwing will ensure that the balls go over to the right-hand side.*

---

## TROUBLESHOOTING

● The most likely problem is that the balls will collide. To remedy this, concentrate on the throws. The balls must move about six inches (fifteen centimeters) to the right before they land.

## TIPS AND HINTS

● Rotate the wrist clockwise as far as possible when throwing to make sure that the balls are thrown slightly to the right. Keep the throws at least sixteen inches (forty centimeters) above head height, but not more than three and a half feet (one hundred centimeters).

### The next challenge:

Try going into three balls in one hand from a cascade. Throw a ball from your right hand slightly to the right, and a bit higher than usual, then throw a high ball from the left (again aiming past your right hand). Then go into the pattern of three in one hand.

## THREE IN ONE HAND *Tricks*

### Cascade

*Throw the balls from two distinct positions, left and right. The back toss from the left-hand side can be made easier by twisting the wrist as the throw is made. It helps to keep the pattern very narrow.*

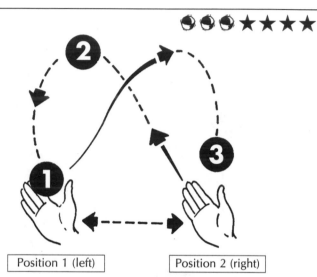

Position 1 (left)     Position 2 (right)

### Columns

*Start toward the inside of your juggle space and work out. Throw from three distinct positions, keeping the throws vertical. To achieve this trick you have to move your hand very fast!*

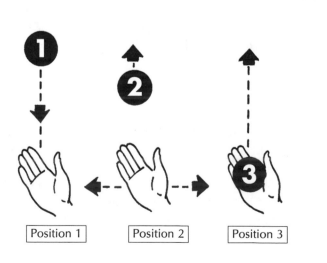

Position 1     Position 2     Position 3

# THREE-BALL FLASHY START

*Skill Rating*  ●●● ★

**1** Hold two balls in your right hand like this to enable you to throw and split them.

**2** Throw and split balls 1 and 2 while holding ball 3 in your left hand.

**3** Throw ball 3 up the center of the pattern, catch balls 1 and 2 and go straight into the cascade.

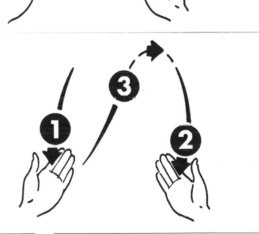

## TROUBLESHOOTING

● The biggest problem is ball 3 colliding with the other two balls. Make sure when you throw balls 1 and 2 that you are creating a big enough gap to throw ball 3 through.

## TIPS AND HINTS

● Practice throwing and splitting the two balls from your right hand. Slightly twisting the wrist as you throw can help, and also throwing them high allows them to split more and look more effective.

# FOUR-BALL FOUNTAIN

*Basic Move*

*Skill Rating*

N ow, let's move on to four balls! The first pattern to master is the fountain: each hand juggles two balls, and the balls **do not cross**.

**1** *To start, just hold two balls in one hand.*

**2** *Throw ball 1 from near to the body and as it peaks throw ball 2. Move your hand outward about four inches to catch the incoming ball 1. Keep this pattern going. Once you have mastered this with one hand do exactly the same thing with the other hand.*

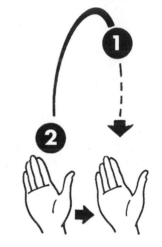

**3** *Now, holding two balls in each hand, throw balls 1 and 3 simultaneously. As they peak throw balls 2 and 4 simultaneously. The balls should travel in a tight circular pattern. The left-hand balls will travel counterclockwise, and the right-hand balls clockwise. This is called the "on-sync" fountain.*

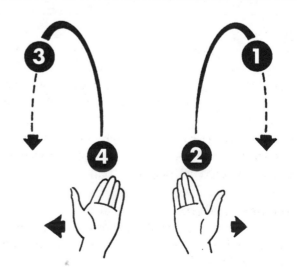

# FOUR-BALL FOUNTAIN *Audience View*

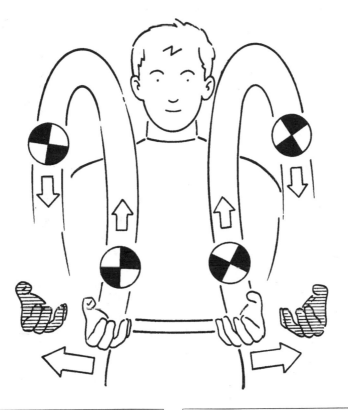

| **TROUBLESHOOTING** | **TIPS AND HINTS** |
|---|---|

● The major difficulty you may encounter is that the balls collide in the center. If you twist the wrists slightly to point outward this will encourage the balls to travel in an outward circle.

● If the balls are not being caught and thrown simultaneously then you are not throwing to the same height.

● Before working on the trick as a whole, practice simultaneously throwing one ball from each hand to the same height and catching them.

● Use two balls of one color in the right hand and two balls of a different color in the left hand. This helps to keep the two sides separate in your mind.

### The next challenge:
Once you have learned this pattern on-sync (simultaneously), try experimenting with throwing it off-sync. You need to be able to do both to progress to more advanced tricks.

# CENTER CROSS

*Basic Move*

*Skill Rating*

**1** *Hold two balls in each hand.*

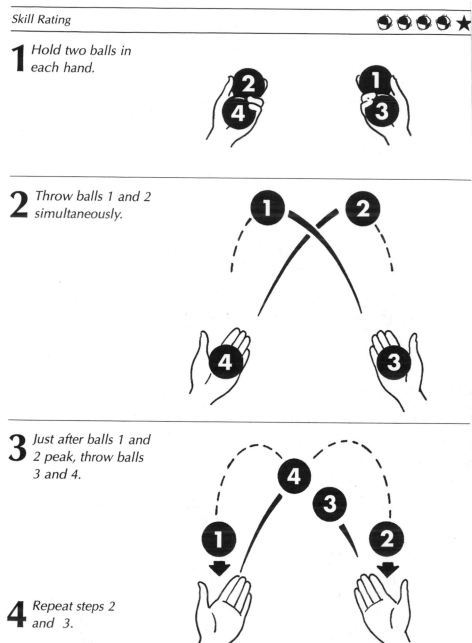

**2** *Throw balls 1 and 2 simultaneously.*

**3** *Just after balls 1 and 2 peak, throw balls 3 and 4.*

**4** *Repeat steps 2 and 3.*

## The next challenge:

Go into this pattern from the on-sync pattern.

# CENTER CROSS *Audience View*

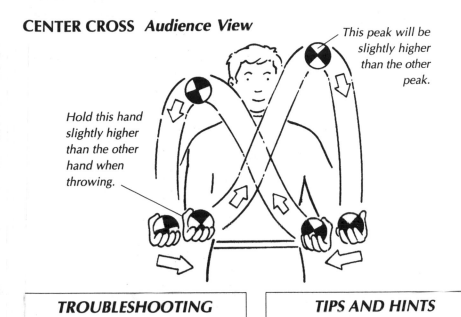

This peak will be slightly higher than the other peak.

Hold this hand slightly higher than the other hand when throwing.

---

| **TROUBLESHOOTING** | **TIPS AND HINTS** |
|---|---|
| ● If you are experiencing midair collisions, then there is not enough of a height difference between your two hands when you are releasing the balls. | ● Hold one hand slightly higher than the other. |

## CENTER CROSS *Tricks*

### Rainbow Cross                    ✪✪✪✪ ★★

*This trick is similar to the three-ball rainbow cross, but the two balls are thrown simutaneously up the center while the other two cross over the top.*

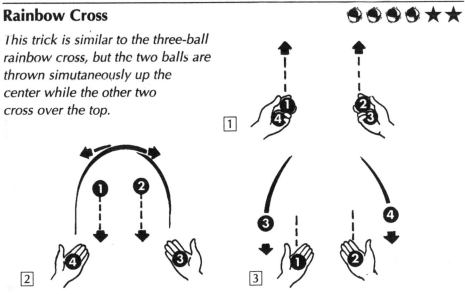

# FOUR-BALL MULTIPLEX CASCADE

*Skill Rating* 🌑🌑🌑🌑 ★★

**1** Throw ball 1 to the left.

**2** Throw balls 3 and 4 simultaneously, so that they split, with ball 4 going toward your right hand, and ball 3 returning to the left.

**3** Throw ball 2 toward the left. Catch ball 1 and then ball 3 in your left hand. Catch ball 4 in your right hand.

Continue with your left hand throwing a split of two balls (as it did in step 2) and your right hand throwing a low ball. Ball 3 is always thrown and caught by the left hand in a split, and the other three balls circulate.

### The next challenge:
While juggling four balls off-sync, catch and hold two balls in your left hand, throw one ball from your right hand to your left, then go into the multiplex cascade.

## FOUR-BALL MULTIPLEX CASCADE *Audience View*

*Twisting the wrist as you release the two balls helps to split them.*

---

## TROUBLESHOOTING

● If the balls are not separating properly, make sure they are level in your hand before you throw them.

*Correct*

*Incorrect*

## FOUR-BALL MUTIPLEX CASCADE *Tricks*

*If you learn to split with your right hand as well, you can alternate left- and right-hand splits for a symmetrical pattern.*
*The throws are as follows:*
*1. Your right hand throws one ball toward the left.*
*2. Throw a split from your left hand.*
*3. Throw a ball to the right from your left hand.*
*4. Throw a split from your right hand. Repeat steps 1 to 4.*

# FOUR-BALL STACKED CASCADE

*Skill Rating*  ◔◔◔◔ ★★★

**1** Hold three balls in your right hand, and one ball in your left.

**2** Throw ball 1 to the left.

**3** Throw ball 2 to the right, and catch ball 1.

**4** Throw balls 3 and 4 simultaneously to the left, so they split vertically (stack). Catch ball 2.

**5** *Throw ball 1 to the right. Catch ball 4 first, then ball 3 in your left hand. This is effectively a three-ball cascade pattern with balls 3 and 4 counting as one ball.*

*To continue, keep throwing right then left, always throwing balls 3 and 4 simultaneously.*

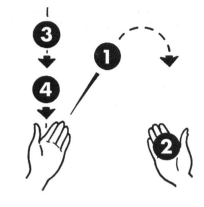

## FOUR-BALL STACKED CASCADE *Audience View*

*The two stacked balls.*

### The next challenge:
Try going into a four-ball stacked cascade from the off-sync fountain, and then go back to the fountain after a few throws.

---
**TIPS AND HINTS**
---

● Flick the wrist upward as you release balls 3 and 4; this makes them stack nicely.

## FOUR-BALL STACKED CASCADE *Tricks*

*Practically any three-ball trick can be attempted using this method.*
*Particularly recommended tricks are:*
*1. Under the leg — with the stacked pair being thrown under.*
*2. Columns — with the center ball being replaced by the stacked pair.*
*3. Mills' Mess — try replacing ball 1 with the stacked pair.*

# FOUR-BALL HALF SHOWER   *Basic Move*

*Skill Rating*   🌐🌐🌐🌐★★★

**1** Throw ball 1 to the left, just above head height. A split second later, throw ball 2 to the right at about chin height.

**2** After a slight pause, throw ball 3 to the left, just above head height, and throw ball 4 to the right at about chin height.

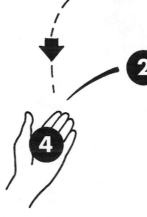

Note: The throws should be made with the cadence 1, 2, pause, 1, 2, pause; 1 represents a throw to the right at just above head height, and 2 represents a throw to the left at chin height.

# HALF SHOWER *Audience View*

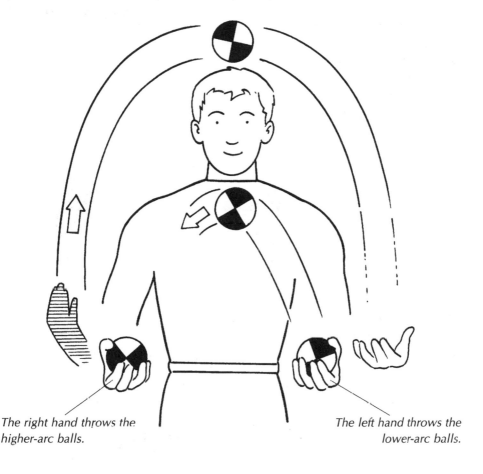

The right hand throws the higher-arc balls.

The left hand throws the lower-arc balls.

---

## TIPS AND HINTS

● The balls from your left hand follow a lower arc, and the balls from your right hand follow a higher arc. If you make these two arcs almost the same height, you should throw pairs of balls almost simultaneously. If you make the higher arc three times the height of the lower arc (height measured above the hands), then the timing of your throws will be similar to the steady left/right of the three-ball cascade. Vary the height, and notice how the timing changes.

● Some people find it easier to throw the first two balls simultaneously and then slip into the correct timing.

# FOUR-BALL SHOWER

*Basic Move*

*Skill Rating*  ◉◉◉◉★★★

**1** Hold three balls in your right hand, and one in your left.

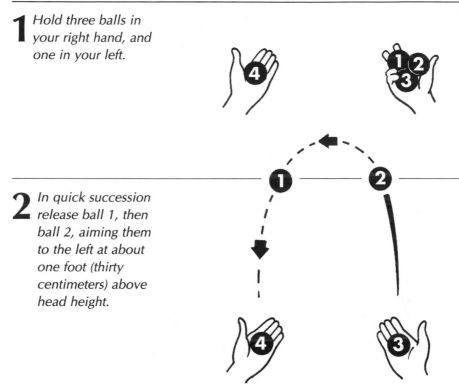

**2** In quick succession release ball 1, then ball 2, aiming them to the left at about one foot (thirty centimeters) above head height.

**3** As with the three-ball shower, spring the ball in your left hand across to your right hand and launch the ball from your right hand simultaneously over toward your left.

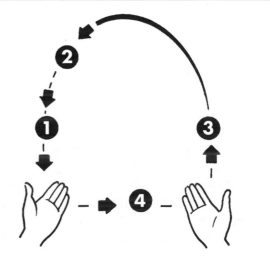

*Repeat step 3 to maintain the shower pattern.*

## FOUR-BALL SHOWER *Audience View*

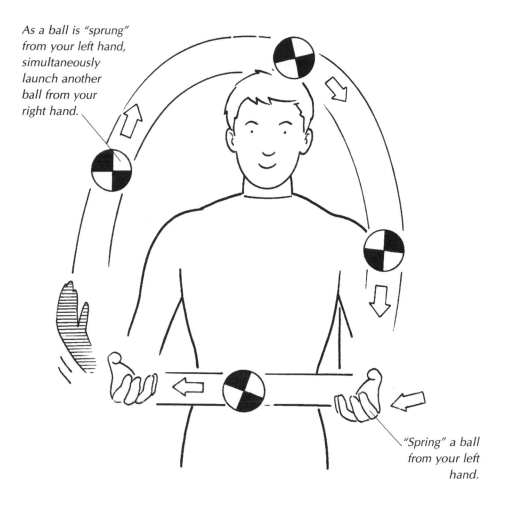

*As a ball is "sprung" from your left hand, simultaneously launch another ball from your right hand.*

*"Spring" a ball from your left hand.*

| TROUBLESHOOTING | TIPS AND HINTS |
|---|---|

● You may find it difficult to stop the balls from colliding in the air. Angle the palm of your right hand at 45 degrees to the ground to ensure that all the throws go far enough to the left. Concentrate on not letting the balls move forward at all.

● Release the first two balls quickly before falling into a comfortable timing.

● Practicing a very low and fast three-ball shower may also help you get used to the feel of the four-ball shower.

### The next challenge:

While doing a four-ball (off-sync), throw a ball slightly higher than usual from your left hand, straight up the left-hand side. Throw the next ball from your right hand toward the left-hand side, and go straight into the shower pattern.

## FOUR-BALL SHOWER  *Tricks*

### High Ball

While showering, throw one ball from your right hand about two feet (sixty centimeters) higher than usual. Throw the next ball from your right hand lower than usual, and then go back to the normal four-ball shower height.

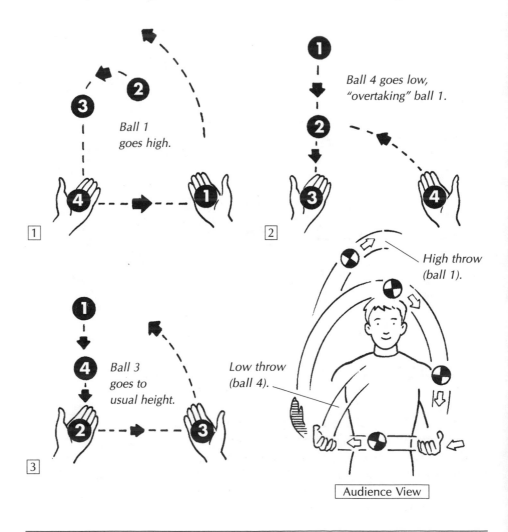

# FOUR-BALL MILLS' MESS    *Basic Move*

*Skill Rating*      🌑🌑🌑🌑★★★★★★

**1** To build up to this very difficult pattern it is necessary to master the three-ball Mills' Mess plus two other patterns, the first being the reversed four-ball off-sync fountain.

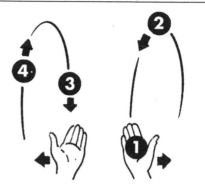

**2** Now change that reversed off-sync fountain into a reversed **crossed** off-sync fountain.

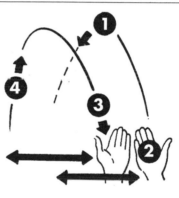

**3** You now need to combine elements from the previous two patterns with the crossed-arm throws that make a Mills' Mess pattern. An important rule to remember about the four-ball Mills' Mess is that the balls **do not swap hands**—the two balls that start in the right hand always remain in the right hand. So ball 1 from the right hand is thrown toward the left, quickly followed by ball 2. The right hand then moves across to the left (crossing arms), catches ball 1 and throws it back to the right, then catches ball 2 and throws that back to the right. The right hand now returns to the right (uncrossing arms) to catch ball 1. The left hand does exactly the opposite with its two balls but one beat out of time (off-sync).

**4** Now is the time to put all the various elements together. A successful four-ball Mills' Mess is dependent on combining the throws and catches described in step 3 with the correct sequence of arm crossovers. This is where your experience of the three-ball Mills' Mess comes into play, as the arm crossover sequence is the same (see pages 37–39).

## FOUR-BALL MILLS' MESS *Audience View*

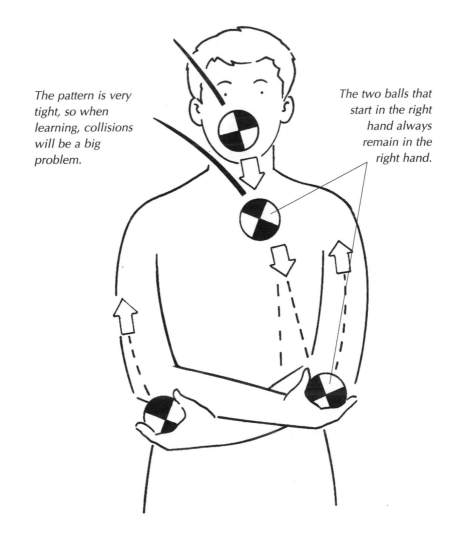

The pattern is very tight, so when learning, collisions will be a big problem.

The two balls that start in the right hand always remain in the right hand.

## TROUBLESHOOTING

● Collisions are the biggest problem with this pattern. It is important to make sure that throws made from a lower arm (in crossed-arm position) are not quite vertical, but slightly back toward the side of the arm that throws them.

## TIPS AND HINTS

● The best tip for doing the four-ball Mills' Mess is not to worry too much about where the balls are going, but to focus on the fact that it feels very much like juggling the three-ball Mess, but faster. If you are very confident with the three-ball mess, then after a few attempts at the four-ball version you will instinctively know if the pattern feels right or wrong.

● When you are juggling the four-ball Mills' Mess it can help if you make a point of swaying the top half of your body in the direction of the arm that is currently crossing on top of the other arm. This has the effect of widening the pattern and reducing collisions.

● Try entering the Mess from both inward fountain and outward fountain (using an over-the-top throw to start the arm crossing movement). Different people find different starts easier.

### Some challenges to consider:

There are many possible variations once this pattern is solid. You can pop the odd ball over the shoulder (best done by a hand just before it starts to cross over the other arm). You can try to shower a ball from one hand to the other at the point where the arms uncross (this is a very fast throw!). Start creating your own variations on the pattern — some beautiful results are possible, but they are not easy! Five-ball Mills' Mess is also possible. It is difficult to describe the moves in stages, but once you are comfortable with the four-ball Mess, and can cascade five balls, try the following:

Cascade five balls. Turn the cascade into a reverse cascade. Start the arm movements for Mills' Mess and you will find it just feels natural — if a little difficult to sustain!

## PLEASE NOTE

● The four-ball Mills' Mess is a **very advanced** juggling pattern. With intermittent practice it could easily take a year or more to master. But by the time you are considering working on this pattern you will have invented some of your own strategies to achieve juggling feats. Use these to overcome the Mills' Mess!

# FIVE-BALL CASCADE

**Basic Move**

*Skill Rating*  🌑🌑🌑🌑🌑★★

For most jugglers, the ultimate in ball juggling is to be able to juggle five balls! As with three balls, the first pattern to master is the cascade. The cascade with five balls, however, is a pattern of great beauty. To successfully juggle five balls your timing must be precise and your accuracy in terms of height and direction must also be excellent. A golden rule about five-ball juggling that can make all the difference when you start is: **it's not that fast!** Slow down, there's plenty of time.

## STARTER TIPS

● Slow down: throwing fast only creates an uncontrollable mess.
● Throw the balls/beanbags to approximately thirty inches (seventy-five centimeters) above your hands.
● Use five different-colored balls/beanbags—this helps your brain to sort out the confusion into a clear pattern.

**1** *Before you attempt five balls you should become very comfortable with the three-ball flash. While cascading three balls, throw them higher than usual in quick succession so your hands are momentarily empty. When the balls approach your hands, catch them and quickly throw them out, again leaving your hands empty. Repeat this until you can keep flashing three balls with little effort. The timing is 1, 2, 3, wait, wait, 1, 2, 3, wait, wait. The two waits will become the other two balls.*

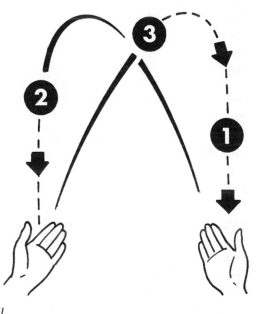

**2** This step is called the controlled drop, and all you are initially doing is concentrating on the throws and not the catches. Hold three balls in your dominant hand and two in the other. In a cascade pattern, throw **as slowly as you like**, to about thirty inches (seventy-five centimeters) above your hands. If the balls drop in two clusters on either side of your feet, your accuracy of throw is good. Listen to the sound of the dropping balls, if there are equal gaps between the drops, your timing is good.

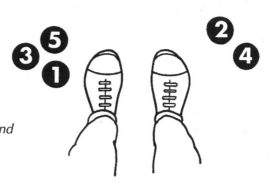

**3** Work on your timing and accuracy using the controlled drop. When you feel confident, start to catch the balls, simply that. Don't attempt to throw the balls again; the aim of this step is to throw and catch five balls. If everything is working correctly you should catch the first ball just before throwing the fifth.

**4** Now that you can throw and catch five balls on a regular basis, start trying to add just one or more throws before you catch all the balls. Always try to add just one more throw than the last attempt. Still practice the controlled drop now and again.

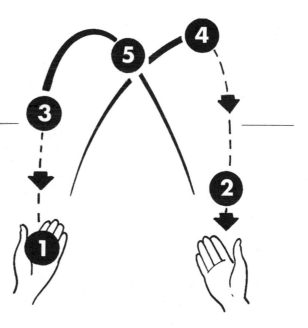

When you can do fifteen throws on a regular basis move on to step 5.

**5** *To master continuous five-ball cascading you must start varying your pattern between absurdly high to ridiculously low, arm-splitting wide to perilously narrow, and everything in between. The reason for this is that at the fifteen-throw stage you can cope with the pattern as long as it is perfect, but one faulty throw and you've had it! When practicing different heights and widths your brain learns how to react to different situations and can recover from the poor throws that would otherwise wreck your pattern.*

## TROUBLESHOOTING

● You may be throwing too far forward with one hand. Try juggling with the opposite foot forward: i.e., if you are throwing forward with your left hand, put your right foot forward. This may correct the error. If it doesn't, try to imagine you are aiming balls to land on your own shoulders, not to the hands. This should correct the erroneous throws.

● Other common problems are throwing a ball straight up rather than across, or persistently throwing low with one hand. Look for these problems, as identifying them is most of the way to correcting them.

## TIPS AND HINTS

● Relax your shoulders.

● Try throwing with your arms at different heights.

● Don't hold your breath. Keep breathing deep, even and relaxed.

● Take regular breaks and do something else — your brain is working on the problem when your arms aren't.

● Sometimes practice doesn't seem to make any improvement for the next time you try, but in a week's time you will be much better.

● In the early stages of learning, try not to miss a day's practice, even five minutes a day will help.

## ONE HUNDRED PLUS THROWS

So you can get to thirty or forty throws practically every attempt, but something is going wrong. You can't yet reach one hundred throws, and you are not totally confident with five balls.

**Problem:** If you've achieved forty throws your timing and positional accuracy are fine, but the problem stems from lack of strength in your arms. Your arms are not capable of something your brain is.

**Solution:** Buy some wrist weights of about one pound each. These are easily available from fitness stores. A few minutes practicing with weights is more productive than an hour without. This extra strength that will come after only a few days of ten to fifteen minutes' practice will allow you to juggle five balls for long periods of time without a drop.

## FIVE-BALL CASCADE *Audience View*

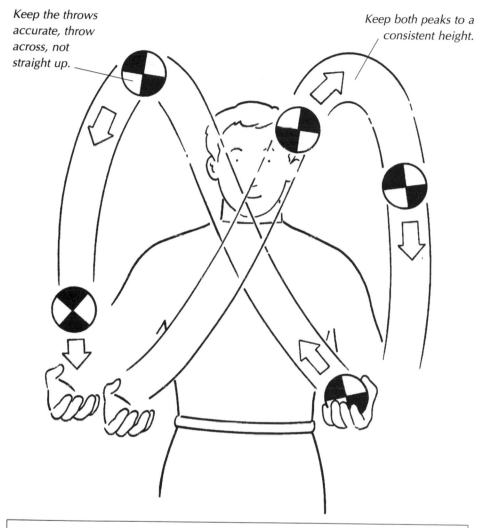

Keep the throws accurate, throw across, not straight up.

Keep both peaks to a consistent height.

---

### A FINAL TIP

It may sound crazy, but to go on and reach higher targets why not start juggling seven balls—yes seven! It is possible. You juggle with seven in just the same way as you do with five. It gives you a feel for seven and makes five feel much easier! For seven-ball juggling, hold three balls in each hand and place the seventh ball on top of the three balls in your dominant hand. This ball is thrown first.

---

# FIVE-BALL STACKED CASCADE  *Basic Move*

*Skill Rating*

**1** Hold three balls in your right hand, and two balls in your left. Your right hand throws ball 1 in a normal cascade throw.

**2** From here on, balls 2 and 3, and balls 4 and 5 are thrown as stacked pairs. The timing is the same as the three-ball cascade.

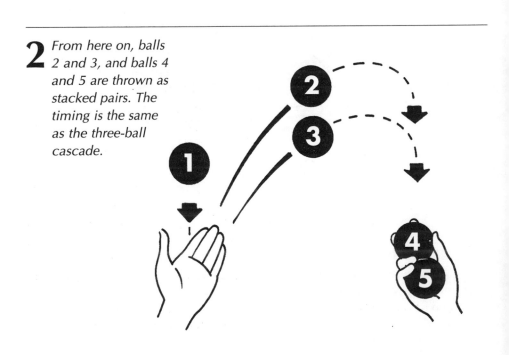

# FIVE-BALL STACKED CASCADE *Audience View*

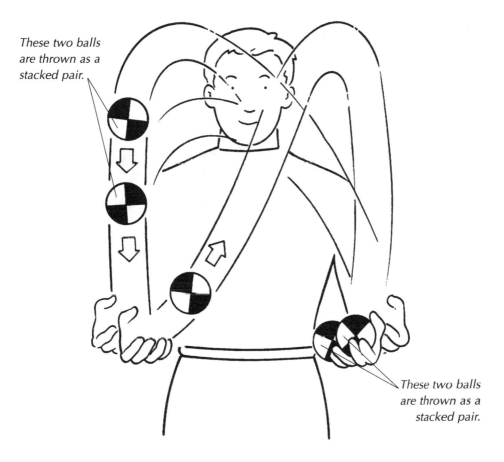

These two balls are thrown as a stacked pair.

These two balls are thrown as a stacked pair.

---

| **TROUBLESHOOTING** | **TIPS AND HINTS** |
| --- | --- |

● If you are having problems with catching the stacks, then go back to the four-ball version, and practice some more.

● If your stacked throw is not perfect, concentrate on catching the lower ball, then quickly move to scoop up the higher ball. Steady the lower ball with your little finger, leaving the rest of your hand to catch the higher one.

### The next challenge:
Why not try a six-ball cascade? Every throw is a stack of two balls. Hold four balls in your right hand and two in your left to start.

## FIVE-BALL STACKED CASCADE *Tricks*

### Columns ◉◉◉◉◉★★★

*This is quite tricky! Throw the lone ball up the center, and then a stack of two balls up each side.*

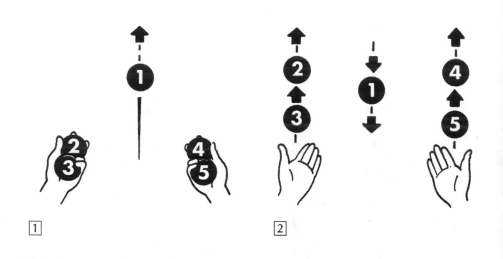

### Rainbow Cross ◉◉◉◉◉★★★★★

*This is a very difficult trick! Four balls need to cross without colliding. First throw the lone ball up the center, then cross the two stacks simultaneously. The main difficulty is not avoiding collisions but making the simultaneous stacked catches.*

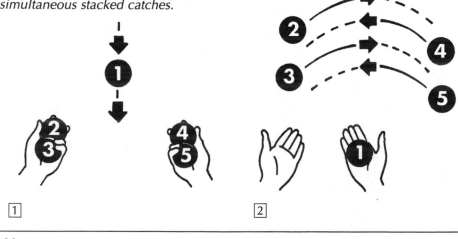

# FIVE-BALL OVER THE TOP    *Basic Move*

*Skill Rating*     ★ ★

**1** While cascading, after your right hand catches a ball, move it slightly to the left.

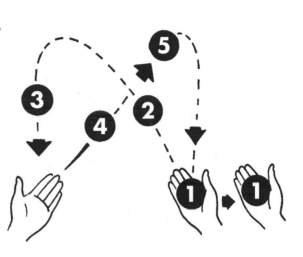

**2** Launch ball 1 over the top of the pattern. Then three cascade throws are made before ball 1 lands:
your left hand throws ball 3;
your right hand throws ball 5;
your left hand throws ball 2.
You may need to move your left hand leftward slightly to catch ball 1 when it falls.

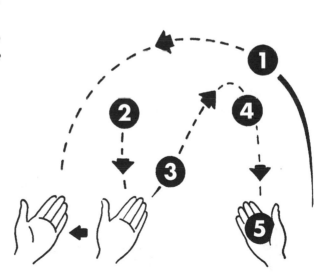

# FIVE-BALL OVER THE TOP *Audience View*

Make sure this over-the-top ball comfortably clears the rest of the pattern.

---

| **TROUBLESHOOTING** | **TIPS AND HINTS** |
|---|---|
| ● Make sure that your right hand moves out far enough so that the over-the-top ball clears the rest of the pattern. | ● Your right hand needs to move out, throw and return to its usual position very quickly, otherwise you will drop an incoming ball. |

### The next challenge:
You could try sending the over-the-top ball the other way — i. e., from left to right.

## FIVE-BALL OVER THE TOP *Tricks*

*Do not attempt either of the following tricks until you can do about 100 to 150 throws of the five-ball cascade without dropping.*

### Tennis ●●●●●★★★

*One ball can be thrown back and forth across the top of the pattern.*

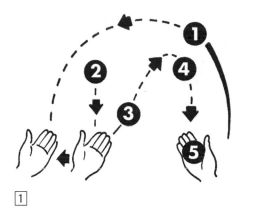

### Half Shower ●●●●●★★★

*Throw every ball from one side over the top of the pattern, creating two arcs. Your timing will alter slightly to accommodate the change in pattern. The cadence is left right, left right, etc., with the left and right being almost simultaneous.*

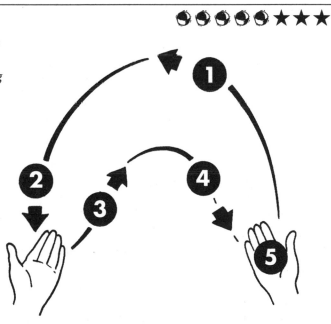

# 2

# CLUB JUGGLING

## Three-Club Juggling

Once you have mastered the three-ball cascade you can use exactly the same pattern to juggle three clubs. The main difference between ball juggling and club juggling is that clubs spin when thrown.

When you start club juggling you will undoubtedly drop your clubs a lot, so in the first instance buy some strong, robust clubs. Many companies now manufacture clubs specifically for learning: they usually have softer handles, which means beginner's errors hurt less. As you become more proficient you may find these "learner" clubs start to become restrictive. You can then change to a more "professional" club that will be weighted differently, to spin easier, enabling you to throw multispins effortlessly and indulge in much more complicated patterns. You will also find that the more professional clubs require far less energy to juggle.

Finally it is worth remembering that out-of-control flying clubs can cause damage. So to start with consider practicing outside in a open space. If you have to practice inside, make sure that you have enough room around and above you and that you are not near anything breakable!

# THREE-CLUB CASCADE

*Basic Move*

*Skill Rating*                                    3 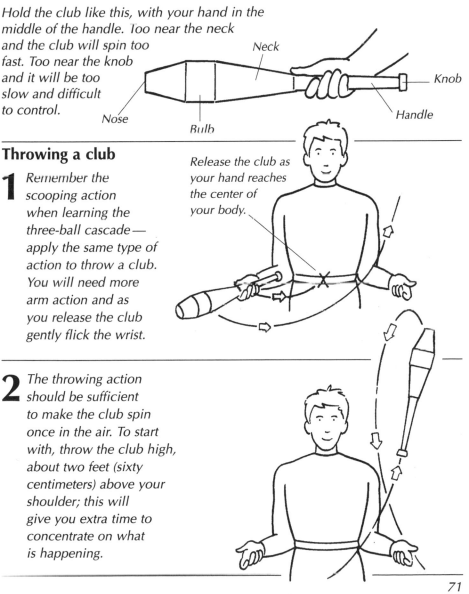 ★

The three-club cascade pattern is exactly the same as the three-ball cascade pattern, but to achieve this with clubs it is essential to be able to hold, throw and catch the clubs correctly.

## Holding a club

*Hold the club like this, with your hand in the middle of the handle. Too near the neck and the club will spin too fast. Too near the knob and it will be too slow and difficult to control.*

Neck

Knob

Nose

Handle

Bulb

## Throwing a club

**1** *Remember the scooping action when learning the three-ball cascade — apply the same type of action to throw a club. You will need more arm action and as you release the club gently flick the wrist.*

*Release the club as your hand reaches the center of your body.*

**2** *The throwing action should be sufficient to make the club spin once in the air. To start with, throw the club high, about two feet (sixty centimeters) above your shoulder; this will give you extra time to concentrate on what is happening.*

## Catching a club

**1** *Catch the club with the other hand, and aim to catch it with your hand in the same position on the club as it was when you threw it. To absorb the impact of the catch, move your hand down with the club as you catch it. If thrown and caught correctly the club will be in a mirror position of its starting point.*

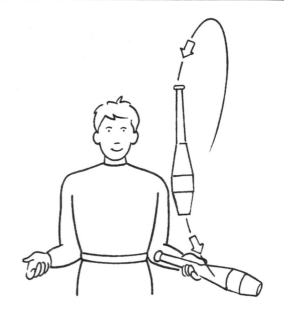

**2** *Repeat this in the opposite direction and slowly build up a rhythm of throwing one club from hand to hand with a single spin each time.*

## Two clubs

**1** *In the same way you progressed to two balls, try two clubs, starting with a club in each hand. The main problem you will encounter is the clubs colliding in midair. To avoid this make sure you throw both clubs to the same height and wait for the first one to reach its highest point before throwing the second.*

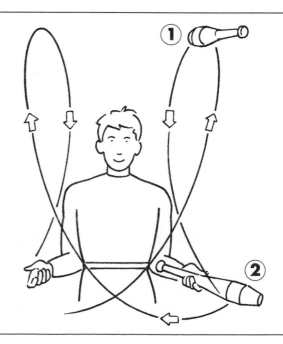

## Three clubs

**1** Hold two clubs in one hand and one club in the other.

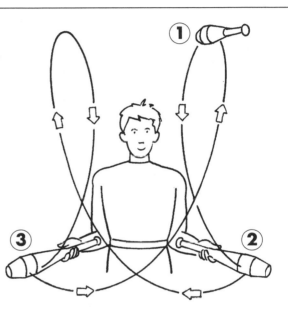

Extend your index finger along the neck of club 1; this will help to launch it.

**2** Launch club 1 first and go into the cascade pattern — the throws and timing are exactly the same as the three-ball cascade, and remember each club spins only once as it is thrown from one hand to the other. To start, you will encounter problems: just stop, think about it, break down the problem and try again!

| TROUBLESHOOTING | TIPS AND HINTS |
|---|---|

● If you are not holding the clubs correctly, as shown on page 71, you will not have maximum control over the clubs when throwing them and if not caught correctly the next throw will possibly suffer.

● Collisions tend to be a big problem when starting. The clubs need to be thrown to the same height, but collisions also occur if you are juggling a too narrow pattern. If this is the case hold your arms farther apart and throw the clubs across more.

● If you are encountering problems when moving on to two or three clubs, go back a step, build up a bit more confidence and then try again.

● Juggle high to start with; this will give you more time. Then slowly bring the pattern down, and as you become more confident you will be able to cascade well below head height.

● Don't throw too fast! One of the joys of club juggling is the slow, steady rhythm. As you juggle try counting to yourself — 1, 2, 3, 1, 2, 3, 1, 2, 3, etc.

# DOUBLE SPINS

*Basic Move*

Skill Rating                                      3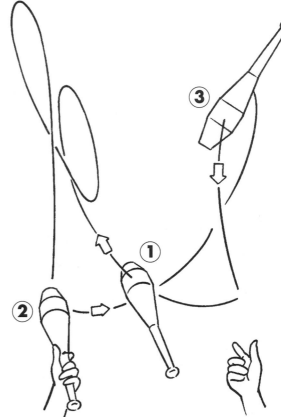

**This is an important trick**. Learn it before you attempt any of the other club tricks.

**1** Your right hand throws club 1 with a double spin and catches club 3. After a slight pause, club 2 is thrown with a single spin and club 1 is caught.

**2** Single-spin cascade continues.

Note: Make the double spin about one foot (thirty centimeters) above head height.

---

| **TROUBLESHOOTING** | **TIPS AND HINTS** |
|---|---|

● If you keep catching the bulb instead of the handle, practice with one club some more.

● If you are having problems continuing with the cascade after the double spin, you are probably not pausing enough.

● Practice throwing and catching doubles with one club before trying a double in a cascade. Do not use your wrist to gain extra spin: throw the club higher, and it will automatically spin more because it is in the air longer.

# DOUBLE SPINS *Audience View*

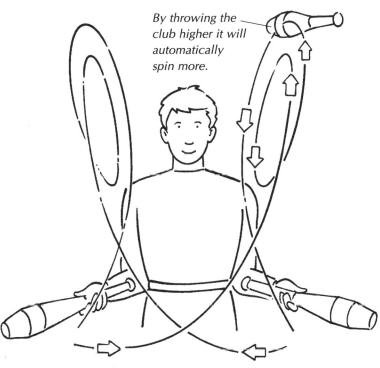

By throwing the club higher it will automatically spin more.

### The next challenge:

Practice throwing every club from one hand with a double spin. Now learn to do doubles with the other hand. Finally, try throwing doubles "solidly" from both hands.

## MULTISPIN *Tricks*

### Triples
 **★★**

*Repeat the trick detailed above but doing triple spins instead of double spins!*

### Double/triple/double/single
 **★★★**

*This trick is difficult and not much to look at, but excellent practice for multiple spins. While cascading in singles, throw three doubles in a row and then immediately follow with three triples. Drop back to doubles for another three throws, and finally return to singles.*

# CHINS

*Basic Move*

Skill Rating

3 ⬤▭▬━● ★★★

**1** While cascading, throw one club slightly higher than the usual from your left hand (use less wrist action, so it spins slower and only does a single spin). Let the club in your right hand slip down slightly so that the knob is held. Very quickly raise the club and place it on the chin. Push it to the left slightly so it falls off and drops into the left hand without spinning. The right hand catches the high club at about head height.

To balance a club, focus on the nose of the club and use slight movements of your head to compensate for it leaning in different directions.

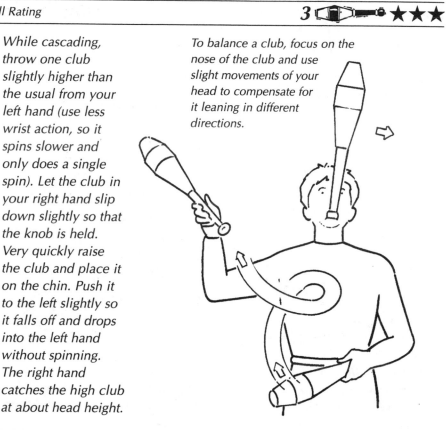

---

| TROUBLESHOOTING | TIPS AND HINTS |
|---|---|
| ● Give yourself time to bring your hand up to your chin by doing a nice, slow, floaty, single spin from your left hand immediately prior to the "chin." | ● Practise the chin movement with just one club to start. Use your first finger to push the club to the left so that it falls correctly. |

## CHINS  *Tricks*

### Chins to balance

3 ⬤▭▬━● ★★★★

*Here's a flash little routine. Chin several clubs in a row before balancing one club on your chin for a few seconds. Knock this club off your chin into your left hand with the bulb of the club that is held in your right hand. This club should do a single spin.*

# KICKUP

*Basic Move*

*Skill Rating*

3 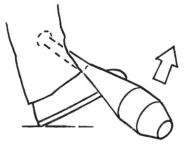 ★★

**1** Place a club on your right foot, with the handle pointing between your legs, and overhanging the foot by about four inches (ten centimeters).

**2** In one movement point your right foot toward your left and swiftly raise your right foot. The club's handle should get momentarily caught in the angle between your foot and your shin, and then spin out, doing a single spin before being caught in your right hand.

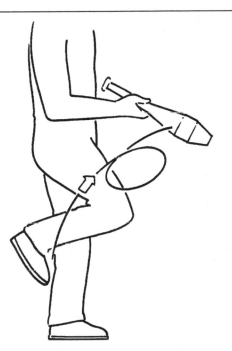

| TROUBLESHOOTING | TIPS AND HINTS |
|---|---|

● Experiment by varying the angle of your foot to your leg.

● Do not wear boots or large sneakers to learn this trick. Lightweight canvas deck shoes are probably the easiest to kick up with.

● Twist your right foot as far counterclockwise as you can.

● Keep as small an angle between your foot and your leg as possible.

### The Kickup — the next challenge:

The kickup is a versatile maneuver, and a valuable addition to your repertoire. You can use it to hide mistakes in a routine, such as dropping a club: with one club in each hand, kick up the dropped club. When it approaches hand level, throw the club in your right hand toward the left with a single spin, catch the kicked up club, and continue to cascade.

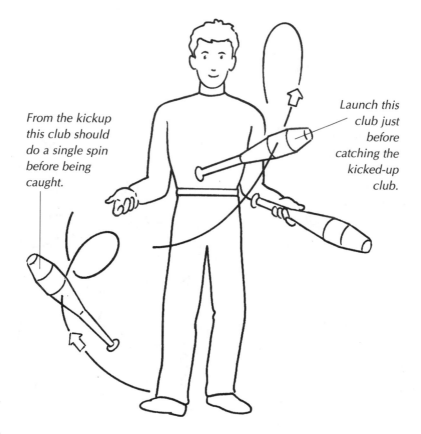

From the kickup this club should do a single spin before being caught.

Launch this club just before catching the kicked-up club.

## KICKUP  *Tricks*

### The drop-kickup

 ★★★

*Practice dropping a club from a cascade onto your foot. Learn to place it so that it is in a position to be kicked straight back up into a cascade. Some people prefer to spin the club onto the foot, slide it down the leg, or just a straight drop. Try a few methods and pick one that you like.*

# FLOURISH

*Skill Rating*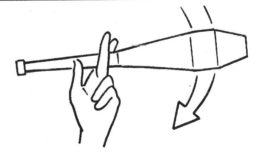

**1** *While juggling a three-club cascade, catch one club as shown with your hand upward.*

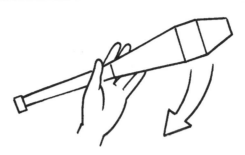

**2** *Let the club swing around. At this point your other hand should throw a double spin club back to the same hand.*

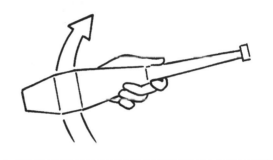

**3** *Let the club continue to spin, now on the other side of the arm, helped by the middle finger.*

**4** *The club will finish its spin and be ready to be thrown from this position. At this point resume the three-club cascade.*

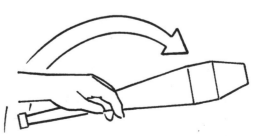

## THE FLOURISH *Audience View*

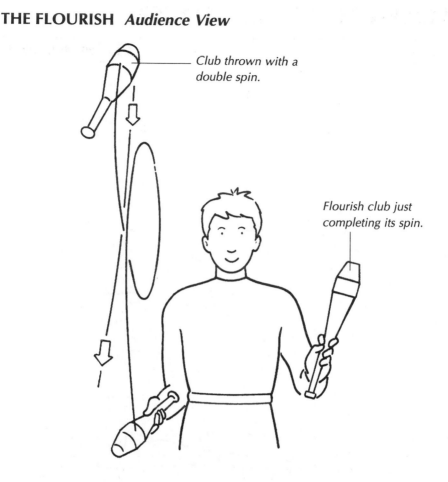

Club thrown with a double spin.

Flourish club just completing its spin.

---

### TROUBLESHOOTING

● If your are having trouble catching the club or performing the flourish quickly enough within a cascade, then practice the catch and flourish maneuvers repeatedly on their own.

### TIPS AND HINTS

● This trick cannot be performed within an ordinary cascade — there is not enough time. Create time for it by making a double-spin throw from the other hand; to return to the same hand, complete the flourish then resume the cascade.

### The next challenge:

Learn to flourish with the other hand, then try a pattern that alternates left- and right-hand flourishes.

# THREE-CLUB FLASH FINISH

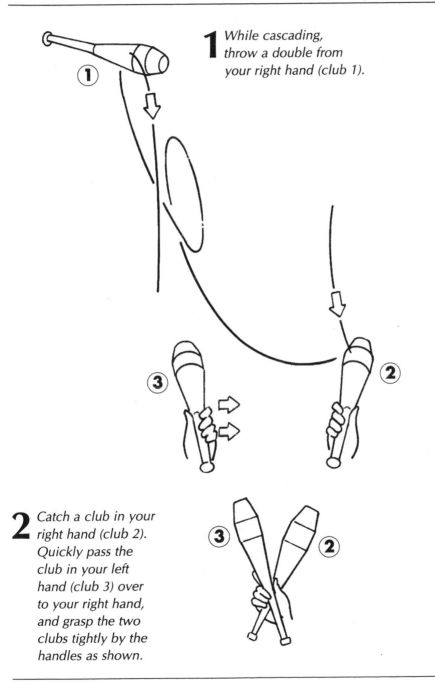

**1** While cascading, throw a double from your right hand (club 1).

**2** Catch a club in your right hand (club 2). Quickly pass the club in your left hand (club 3) over to your right hand, and grasp the two clubs tightly by the handles as shown.

**3** *Hold the V upright and catch the falling club (club 1) by trapping its knob in between the other two clubs.*

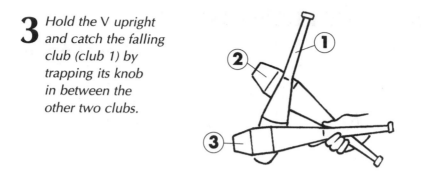

## THREE-CLUB FLASH FINISH *Audience View*

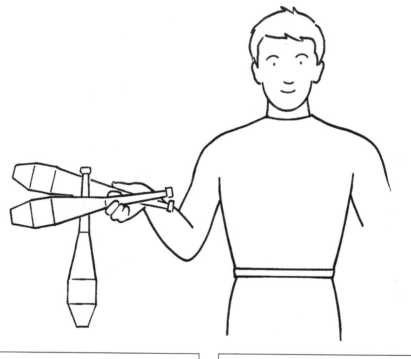

| TROUBLESHOOTING | TIPS AND HINTS |
|---|---|
| ● You will have to experiment with creating a V of the correct angle to catch the falling club. | ● Throw the double a little higher than you normally would, and trap just below head height. |

### The next challenge:
Try trapping a club from a double back cross (see balls) or from a triple spin.

# FOUR-CLUB FOUNTAIN

*Basic Move*

*Skill Rating*

4  ★

The four-club fountain is the same pattern as used in the four-ball fountain, but juggling four clubs is a lot more difficult. So before you attempt this move you should have mastered the four-ball fountain and be reasonably competent with juggling three clubs.

**1** *As with the four ball pattern just concentrate on one hand first. Hold two clubs in one hand.*

**2** *To create enough time and space to juggle two clubs in one hand you will have to use **double spins**. Throw club 1; as it peaks, throw club 2 and move your hand out to catch the incoming club 1. Keep this pattern going. Once you feel confident with one hand, start working on the other hand.*

**3** *Now holding two clubs in each hand, go into the four-club fountain following similar instructions as the four-ball fountain (page 44), but concentrate more on the off-sync pattern.*

## FOUR-CLUB FOUNTAIN  *Audience View*

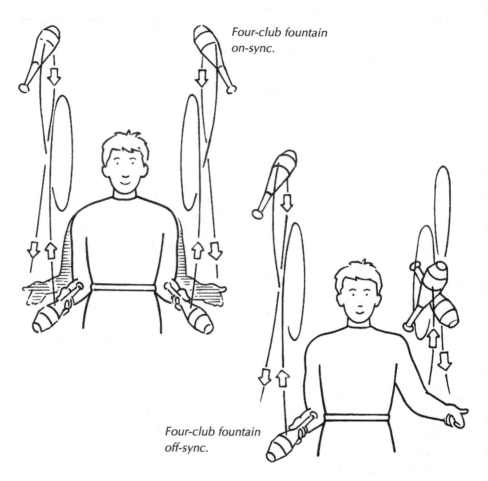

Four-club fountain
on-sync.

Four-club fountain
off-sync.

---

| **TROUBLESHOOTING** | **TIPS AND HINTS** |
|---|---|
| ● Make sure the clubs always point forward while you are juggling two in one hand. It is easy to let them turn slightly and this leads to missed catches and bruised wrists. | ● It is advisable to practice four clubs for short periods and often in the early days, otherwise you could end up with unpleasant bruises. |

### The next challenge:

If you can master the four-club fountain the variations are endless, but try starting with the above patterns in triple spins!

# FOUR-CLUB TRIPLE SINGLE    *Basic Move*

*Skill Rating*                              4 ⬛▬◉ ★★★

This is a kind of lopsided cascade for four clubs. When done correctly it is performed at approximately three-club timing.

**1** *Hold two clubs in each hand. Launch a triple (club 1) from your right hand to your left.*

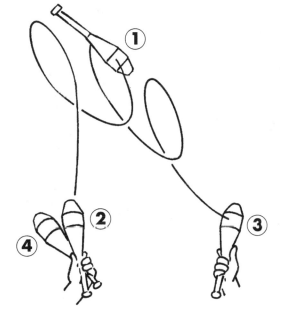

**2** *Launch a single spin (club 2) from your left hand toward the right and then another triple (club 3) from your right. Keep the pattern going with triples from your right hand and singles from your left hand.*

*Note: The paths of the clubs cross.*

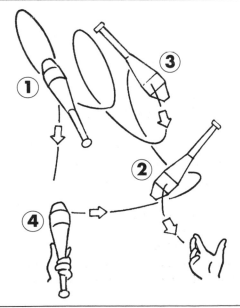

## FOUR-CLUB TRIPLE SINGLE *Audience View*

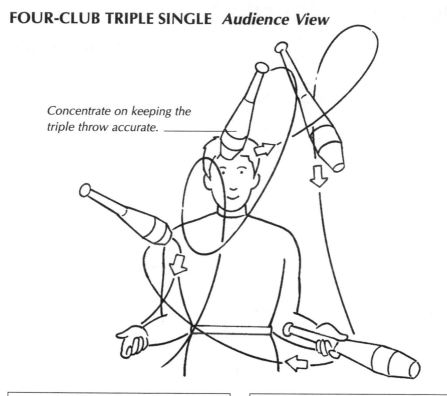

Concentrate on keeping the
triple throw accurate.

| TROUBLESHOOTING | TIPS AND HINTS |
|---|---|

● It is easy to throw the triple either too far to the left, or to throw it slightly forward. Concentrate on placing the triple to avoid running around.

● Focus on the triple and try to forget about the single.

### The next challenge:
When you're confident with triple single, try the harder double-single. The double and the single are thrown almost simultaneously.

## FOUR-CLUB TRIPLE SINGLE *Tricks*

### Body throws                                          4 ★★★★

Try substituting an ordinary triple in the triple-single
pattern for a triple throw behind your back, under
your arm, or under your leg. With the back cross,
be particularly careful not to throw the club too
far to the left.

# KICKUP TO FOUR CLUBS     *Basic Move*

*Skill Rating*                          4 🏏▬● ★★★

Cascade three clubs with
the fourth on your right foot.

**1** *Your right hand
throws a double
spin to the left.*

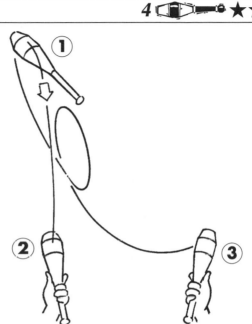

**2** *The fourth club is
kicked up to your
right hand. Your
left hand throws
a double-spin
fountain throw,
followed
immediately by
your right just
before it catches
the kicked-up club.
Continue with an
off-sync fountain
pattern.*

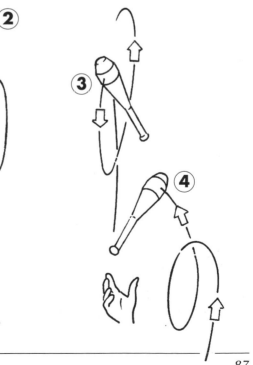

## KICKUP TO FOUR CLUBS (and into an off-sync fountain) *Audience View*

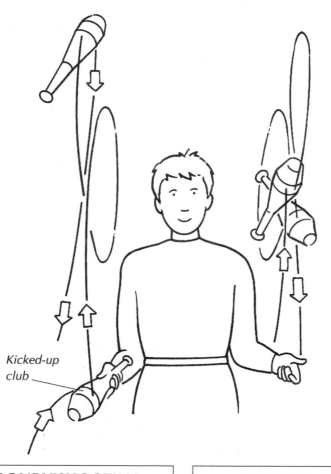

Kicked-up
club

| TROUBLESHOOTING | TIPS AND HINTS |
|---|---|
| ● Experiment with the timing of the kickup. It is crucial that it leaves your right foot just after the first double is thrown. | ● For this trick, you need to be very confident with the kickup, as you can't watch your feet. The more you practice kicking up into the three-club cascade, the easier the four-club version will be. |

### The next challenge:

Try dropping a club onto your foot from a four-club fountain, do a three-club cascade for a couple of throws, and then kick the fourth club back up again. This can be done as a continous pattern.

# FOUR CLUB FINISH

*Skill Rating*

Juggling four clubs can look great but without a good clean finish a routine can be spoiled. Attempting to catch two clubs in each hand can be difficult, so for an effective finish try this...

*Throw a triple spin with the last left-hand club. Catch and hold the two clubs in your right hand. Transfer the club in your left hand over to the right hand and catch the incoming left-hand club with your free left hand.*

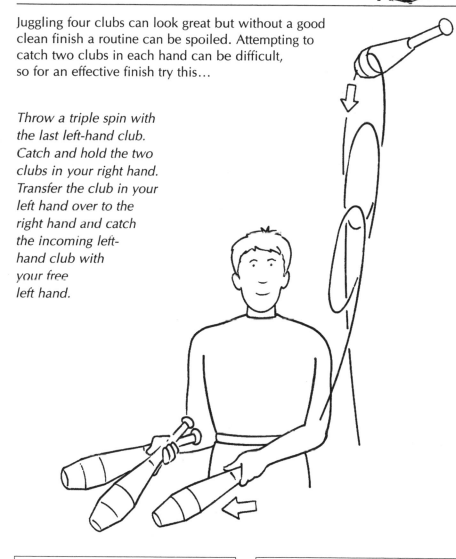

---

| **TROUBLESHOOTING** | **TIPS AND HINTS** |
|---|---|
| ● Plan exactly what you are going to do at the end of the routine and throw the last club high with a triple spin to give yourself time with the other clubs. | ● If you make the last catch look as dramatic as possible it is the perfect end to a routine—take your bow as you make that last catch. |

# FIVE-CLUB CASCADE

*Basic Move*

*Skill Rating*                                           5 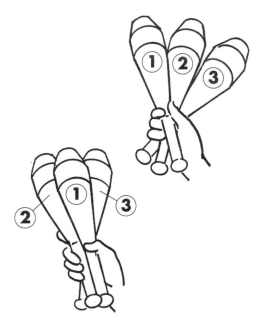 ★

One of the most impressive juggling patterns has to be the five-club cascade—the spectacle and the rhythm of it are what most jugglers aspire to. If you have got this far in the book it should be plain

sailing! Combine the club skills you have already learned with the five-ball cascade instructions (page 60) for the pattern, but ignore the controlled drop section. One of the best pieces of advice is to simply go for it!

*The first problem you will encounter is holding five clubs. Hold three in one hand and two in the other. Launching the first club from the hand holding three clubs will take some practice and you will need to experiment which is the best method for you. Here are two examples of how you could hold them to launch club 1. In both examples use your extended index finger to help give power to the launch.*

---

| TROUBLESHOOTING | TIPS AND HINTS |
|---|---|

● Obviously the biggest problems to start with are collisions. The secret is to throw high, with double spins, and wide. Concentrate on consistent, accurate throws.

● Many problems arise when starting five-club juggling from sheer tiredness; it is hard work and you gradually need to build up to it—take regular rests!

● Many of the tips and hints from the five-ball cascade also apply here, so take a look back at page 62.

● For many jugglers the key to five-club juggling is the rhythm. There is not a lot of time to think about what is going on, but you can concentrate on a steady rhythm—if it helps, count to yourself, *1, 2, 3, 4, 5, 1, 2, 3, 4, 5,* etc....

# FIVE-CLUB CASCADE *Audience View*

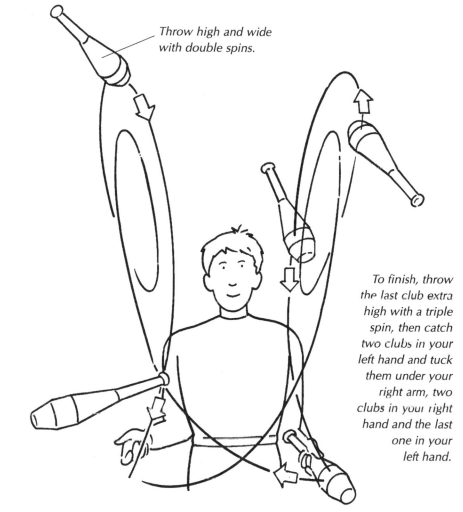

*Throw high and wide with double spins.*

*To finish, throw the last club extra high with a triple spin, then catch two clubs in your left hand and tuck them under your right arm, two clubs in your right hand and the last one in your left hand.*

# FIVE-CLUB CASCADE *Tricks*

Juggling five clubs may seem impressive enough but you can also apply many of the tricks shown in this book to the pattern. Two particular favorites are throwing the occasional club under your leg or behind your back.

## The next challenge:
Try juggling seven clubs! The pattern will be **very** tight. So you will need to use the more controllable "professional" clubs especially made for the "numbers" juggler.

# 3

# INFORMATION

## _____ What Now? _____

You have already mastered a number of tricks in this book, and are experiencing some success with many of the other tricks. However, your juggling now needs some further direction so that it can expand and grow with purpose.

First, see if you can find a local juggling workshop. When you visit it, pester some of the better jugglers present to share some tricks with you. Swap ideas with jugglers of similar ability to yourself and together think up new tricks and challenges. "I know, let's try the six-ball half shower, but with every other throw bouncing off the left knee and behind the right ear!" Search out lots of books on juggling — different authors will describe different tricks in a way that might work better for you. Diversify and try some related arts — for example, diabolo, devil stick, unicycling etc....

For further information about jugglers and juggling in the United States, contact the International Jugglers' Association (IJA), PO Box 3707JB, Akron, OH 44314-3704.

For further information in Europe, contact Kaskade, Annastrasse 7, D-6200 Wiesbaden, Germany.

# Performing

Finally, why not perform your art in front of others — both you and your audience will thoroughly enjoy the experience! Whether you intend to perform onstage or in a friend's living room, a set rehearsed routine is essential to truly impress the onlooker(s).

Write down a list of tricks with which you feel confident. Remember that tricks you can just about do in a relaxed practice session become almost impossible in front of an audience. When you have a list of tricks, put them in an order that you feel will flow. Put something that looks quite difficult near the start of the routine and finish with an impressive trick. Bear in mind that to a nonjuggling audience a simple cascade with an apple, an orange and a pear can look very impressive! Actual skill level does not equal perceived skill level.

It is often easiest and most effective to perform to an upbeat piece of music, but some jugglers use juggling as a platform for comedy. Pick a style you feel happy with and develop a stage personality around it. To get you started, here is a suggestion for a three-ball routine:

**Start:** With two balls in the right hand, one in the left, and do a flashy three-ball start, then go into...

**Columns:** Start with the lone ball in the center for a few throws, then go into the figure of eight and finish this section with a rainbow cross or two.

**Over the top:** Return to the cascade and then throw the odd ball over the top. After a few O.T.T. throws, go into tennis followed by half shower one way, half shower the other way. Throw one of the balls destined for the left hand higher than usual and go straight into the three-ball shower.

**Finish:** While showering, throw one ball high, collect two balls in the right hand, and catch the final ball. Go straight into a bow as the ball is caught.

# Glossary of Terms

**Cadence**  The beat or measure of something rhythmic.

**Claw**  To catch a ball with the palm of the hand facing downward. Depending on the trick, the ball can then be thrown with the the palm facing up or down.

**Dominant hand**  The hand you have most control over; if you are right-handed your right hand is your dominant hand.

**Flash**  Releasing all the balls or clubs in a given pattern in quick succession, leaving the hands empty.

**Jugglespace**  An imaginary frame with a midline, within which the balls or clubs are traveling.

**Multiplex**  When more than one ball is thrown at the same time—for example, when two balls are thrown together to split them.

**Multispin**  When a club spins more than once.

**Numbers juggling**  The pursuit of juggling as many objects as possible at the same time.

**Off-sync pattern**  A pattern with alternate throws.

**On-sync pattern**  A pattern with simultaneous throws.

**Pattern**  The path that the balls or clubs follow.

**Peak**  The highest point of the path of a ball or club.

**Scoop**  The underhand movement of your hand in making a throw, particularly in the cascade pattern.

**Solid**  Juggling a pattern or trick reliably and for a significant duration—for example, if you can juggle the three-ball cascade and regularly manage thirty to fifty consistent throws, your performance would be solid.

**Spring**  To spring a ball is to throw it quickly in a horizontal direction.

**Subordinate hand**  The hand you have least control over; if you are right-handed, your left hand is your subordinate hand.

**Trick**  An extension or variation of the basic pattern.

# Index of Patterns and Tricks